# The Ottoman Empire

While every precaution has been taken in the preparation of this book, the publisher assumes no responsibility for errors or omissions, or for damages resulting from the use of the information contained herein.

THE OTTOMAN EMPIRE

**First edition. January 11, 2024.**



ISBN: 979-8224751211

Written by History Nerds.

# Also by History Nerds

**Ancient Empires**
The Ottoman Empire
Rome: The Rise and Fall

**Celtic Heroes and Legends**
Celtic History
William Butler Yeats: Nobel Prize Winning Poet
Robert the Bruce
Scáthach
Finn McCool
William Wallace: Scotland's Great Freedom Fighter

**Frauen des Krieges**
Boudica: Königin der Icener
Jeanne d'Arc
Irena Sendler

**Great Wars of the World**

World War 1
World War 2
The Napoleonic Wars: One Shot at Glory
The Serbian Revolution: 1804-1835
Peace Won by the Saber: The Crimean War, 1853-1856
The Fiery Maelstrom of Freedom
The Wars of the Roses

**Pirate Chronicles**
Grace O'Malley: The Pirate Queen of Ireland
Blackbeard
William Kidd

**The History of the Vikings**
Vikings
Longships on Restless Seas

**Women of War**
Boudica: Queen of the Iceni
Joan of Arc
Irena Sendler
Virginia Hall
Queen Amanirenas

**World History**
The History of the United Kingdom

The History of Ireland
The History of America
The History of Scotland
The History of Wales


**Standalone**
Grace O'Malley: Die Piratenkönigin von Irland

# Table of Contents

# Introduction

"History is a gallery of pictures in which there are few originals and many copies." Alexis de Tocqueville's words echo with a haunting resonance as one contemplates the vast tableau of the Ottoman Empire. This empire, a colossus that straddled three continents, was as much a cradle of culture and power as it was a mirror of human ambition and frailty. Why should the rise and fall of a bygone empire demand our attention today? The answer lies not merely in the annals of history but in the living veins of our present world. The Ottoman legacy is woven into the very fabric of modern geopolitics, culture, and identity conflicts that shape our daily lives. Spanning over six centuries, the empire's narrative is riddled with paradoxes. How did a small Anatolian beylik expand to rule over lands that once bowed to the might of Byzantines and Pharaohs? And what were the forces, both internal and external, that eventually led to its downfall? As the sun set on the once-majestic Ottoman skyline, shadows of intrigue, warfare, and innovation danced together, whispering secrets that have yet to be fully unraveled. Will you dare to delve into this labyrinth of history, where each corridor promises both enlightenment and enigma? And remember, empires do not crumble in silence—they leave echoes that resonate through the ages, challenging us to listen and learn. But just as the light of understanding seems within grasp, a question emerges from the depths, potent and insistent: Can the rise and fall of an empire like the Ottoman truly be understood, or is it a tale forever shrouded in the mystique of its former glory?

In the labyrinth of history, the echoes of the once-vast Ottoman Empire reverberate with a resonance that calls upon the curious and the scholarly alike. "The past is never dead. It's not even past," William Faulkner famously wrote, and his words are a profound testament to the enduring legacy of empires that once shaped the world. As we delve into the annals of the Ottoman saga, we are reminded that the tapestry of our present is richly embroidered with the threads of its past glories and tribulations.

The relevance of Faulkner's reflection is unmistakable. The Ottoman Empire's influence extends beyond the confines of history books and dusty archives; it permeates the borders of modern nations, the ideologies of current political struggles, and the collective memory of diverse cultures. To understand the present, one must venture into the depths of the past, exploring the rise and fall of a civilization that was as complex as it was captivating.

The story of the Ottomans is marked by a series of dichotomies: the clash between tradition and modernity, the balance of power and grace, and the fine line between conquest and overreach. It is a narrative that raises questions about the nature of power, the inevitability of decline, and the possibility of renewal. By examining the Ottoman Empire's trajectory, we uncover the underlying issues that are as relevant today as they were at the height of the Sultan's power.

It is easy to conceive of the Ottoman Empire in broad strokes—a mighty realm of sultans and viziers, harems and dervishes, conquests and defeats. Yet such a view is limited, neglecting the rich tapestry of human experiences that wove the fabric of Ottoman society. This book seeks to challenge these common beliefs, to dispel the myths, and to offer a nuanced portrait of an empire that was both a force of unparalleled dominance and a mosaic of countless individual stories.

With fresh eyes, we will approach this historical colossus, uncovering insights that traditional narratives have overlooked. We will journey through time, from the empire's audacious beginnings to its drawn-out twilight, examining the pivotal moments and the subtle shifts that shaped its destiny. In doing so, we forge an intellectual bond with the past, acknowledging that the lessons of history are not just to be studied but to be understood and internalized.

Imagine, if you will, the bustling streets of Constantinople at the peak of Ottoman power. The air is thick with the smell of spices and the sounds of many languages. Traders from distant lands barter in the bazaars, scholars debate in the madrasas, and in the sublime magnificence of the Topkapi Palace, a sultan contemplates the expansion of his realm. Such vivid imagery draws us closer to the Ottoman world, stirring our imagination and inviting us to consider how the past continues to mold our present and future.

As we stand at the threshold of this historical expedition, we are compelled to ask: What secrets do the crumbling walls of ancient forts and palaces hold? How did the Ottoman spirit of innovation and adaptation influence the world we know today? And what can the empire's intricate dance with destiny teach us about the rise and fall of civilizations?

This book is not merely a recounting of events; it is an invitation to embark on a journey of discovery. It is a promise that, by understanding the Ottoman Empire's vast narrative, we may glean insights into the broader human experience. So, as we turn the page, let us begin this quest with a mind open to the mysteries and marvels that await. Let the story of the Ottoman Empire be a mirror in which we may see not just the reflection of a past epoch but also the contours of our own time. And let us not forget that every end is also a beginning, for as the final chapter of the Ottoman tale was written, new stories were already unfolding.

Dare to join me, History Nerds, as we unravel the intricate threads of an empire whose shadow looms large over history. Together, we will explore the grandeur and the downfall, the humanity and the ambition, the legacy and the lessons of the Ottoman Empire. And as we tread this path, we will discover that, indeed, the past is not a foreign country but a familiar homeland that continues to shape the world we inhabit.

path, we will discover that, indeed, the past is not a foreign country but a familiar homeland that continues to shape the world we inhabit.

# Foundations of Empire

## Origins of the Osman Dynasty

In the waning years of the 13th century, a whisper of change rustled through the rugged landscape of Anatolia. Here, amidst the chaos of crumbling empires and the clamor of clashing clans, a new force began to stir—a force that would one day carve an empire from the mosaic of fragmented territories and diverse peoples. This force was the Osman Dynasty, a lineage that would lend its name to the sprawling Ottoman Empire.

But what were the currents that brought this dynasty to the forefront of history? The Byzantine Empire, once a bastion of unassailable power, was now a shadow of its former self, weakened by internal strife and external assaults. The Seljuk Sultanate of Rum, having once held sway over Anatolia, was faltering, its grip loosening as it splintered into a constellation of minor principalities and beyliks. In this tumultuous arena, where the old order was disintegrating, the stage was set for the emergence of a new power.

To comprehend our present, we must sift through the sands of time, uncovering the foundations upon which our world is built. The Osman Dynasty's ascent from a modest Anatolian beylik to a mighty empire is not just a tale of conquest and expansion. It is a chronicle of resilience, of strategic alliances, and of visionary leadership that echoes in the chambers of our modern-day struggles for power and influence.

Why, one might ponder, does the genesis of a dynasty that rose over seven centuries ago bear relevance today? The answer lies in the enduring patterns of history—patterns of ambition, struggle, and transformation that repeat themselves across the ages. By understanding the origins of the Osman Dynasty, we gain insight into the forces that shape the rise of powers and the intricate tapestry of human endeavor.

The story of Osman I, the dynasty's eponymous founder, is shrouded in legend and lore. A chieftain of Oghuz Turkic descent, Osman was a leader of vision and valor who capitalized on the power vacuum in the region. Under his command, the Osmanlis, as his followers were known, began to expand their territory, fortifying their position through martial prowess and political marriages.

Consider, for a moment, the audacity of Osman I's dream. In a land rife with uncertainty, what drove this man to envision an empire? Was it the promise of wealth and power, or was it the pursuit of stability and order in a fractured world? These questions invite us to probe deeper into the motivations that fuel the ascent of empires.

As the Osman Dynasty took root, its leaders exhibited an uncanny ability to adapt to the shifting realities of their time. They embraced the diversity of the cultures they encountered, integrating various traditions and practices into the fabric of their burgeoning state. In this synthesis of cultures lay the seeds of an empire that would come to symbolize both the zenith of Islamic civilization and the bridge between East and West.

Now, let us pause and reflect on the significance of this historical tapestry. Envision the vibrant bazaars where ideas, as well as goods, were exchanged, the court where art and architecture flourished, and the battlefields where the fate of nations was decided. What lessons can we draw from this intertwining of human experiences, and how do they resonate with the challenges and opportunities we face in the contemporary world?

As we delve into the narrative of the Osman Dynasty, we embark on a journey that transcends mere historical recounting. We are not only tracing the contours of an empire's birth but also engaging with the perennial questions of leadership, identity, and legacy. Through this exploration, we aspire to not only recount a chapter of history but also to illuminate the enduring human quest for achievement and recognition.

The origins of the Osman Dynasty remind us that history is not a distant relic but a living legacy that influences our daily lives. It shapes the boundaries of nations, the aspirations of leaders, and the identities of peoples. By exploring the roots of the Ottoman Empire, we gain perspective on our own place in the continuum of history—a perspective that is essential for navigating the complexities of our modern existence.

Therefore, let us turn the page with anticipation, ready to uncover the mosaic of events and decisions that gave rise to an empire. An empire that began with the dream of one man, Osman I, and grew to encompass the dreams of countless others. An empire whose story is not confined to the past but continues to shape the narratives of nations and the pulse of history.

Such is the journey upon which we embark—a journey that promises to reveal not only the grandeur and the ambition of the Osman Dynasty but also the intimate human struggles that underpin the saga of empires. Join me as we traverse the annals of time, unraveling the threads of the past to better comprehend our present and imagine our future.

## The First Conquests

THE DAWN OF THE 14TH century witnessed the nascent Osmanli power transitioning from ambition to actuality. Under the shadow of Osman I's dream, the reality of an empire took shape, one conquest at a time. To fully grasp the significance of these early triumphs, one must first understand the strategic acumen and opportunism that marked the rise of the Ottoman Empire.

The capture of Bursa in 1326 stands as a testament to the nascent Ottoman strength. What was it about this city, one might ask, that made its conquest a milestone in the annals of Ottoman history? Bursa, rich and strategically located, was not only a symbol of prestige but also a linchpin in controlling the region. Its fall heralded the transformation of the Ottoman Beylik from a minor principality into a serious contender for power in Anatolia and beyond.

The story of the Ottoman expansion is incomplete without mentioning the fortitude of Osman I's son, Orhan. Under his leadership, the Ottomans saw an era of consolidation and growth. The capture of Bursa, the first major city to fall into Ottoman hands, was a turning point. But what did it herald for the local populace and the wider region? The answer lies in the aftermath of the conquest. Orhan didn't merely subjugate; he revitalized Bursa, making it a capital that attracted merchants, scholars, and artisans, thus seeding the cultural renaissance that would come to define Ottoman rule.

This period of conquest was characterized not only by military victories but also by strategic marital alliances. Orhan's marriage to the daughter of the Byzantine governor of Bilecik was such a move, one that underscored the nuanced diplomacy that often accompanied Ottoman military might. Can one imagine the conversations, the agreements, and the delicate negotiations that took place behind the scenes?

Visualize now the siege of Bursa: the relentless effort of the Ottoman forces, the clash of steel, the cries of warriors, and the silent prayers of the besieged. And then, the moment of surrender, not marked by pillage or destruction, but by a promise of prosperity under a new flag.

But the Ottoman story was not one of unchallenged ascendance. Each victory brought new challenges, from managing newly acquired territories to integrating diverse populations. The Ottomans, however, showed remarkable adaptability, incorporating the cultural and administrative practices of their subjects. Bursa's transformation into a center of Islamic learning and architecture, exemplified by the grand Ulu Cami, is a reflection of this cultural synthesis.

The evolution of the Ottoman military system also played a crucial role in these conquests. The establishment of the Janissaries, an elite corps of soldiers loyal only to the Sultan, revolutionized Ottoman warfare. Consider the sight of these disciplined troops marching to the beat of the war drum, a fearsome and formidable force that struck terror into the hearts of their adversaries.

As the 14th century progressed, so did the Ottoman Empire, with Orhan's successors continuing the legacy of conquest and expansion. These early forays laid the groundwork for a vast empire that would endure for centuries. But what does this tell us about the nature of power and the human ambition to extend one's reach?

The Ottoman Empire's early conquests are not merely a tale of battles won or cities captured; they are a narrative of resilience, strategic vision, and the indomitable human spirit. The capture of Bursa, in particular, symbolizes not only the physical expansion of the Ottoman realm but also the cultural and ideological growth that would come to define this empire.

As we reflect on these formative years, it becomes evident that the seeds of the Ottoman Empire's longevity were sown by its founders. Their ability to dream beyond the horizons of their time, to adapt and evolve, remains a poignant lesson for the leaders of today. What, then, can we learn from the Ottoman blueprint for empire-building? How can the past inform our approach to the geopolitical puzzles of the present?

The Ottoman Empire's story continues to resonate, reminding us that history is not merely a chronicle of conquests but a canvas of human endeavor. It challenges us to look beyond the surface of the past, to understand the complexities and contradictions that shape our world.

So, let us carry forward the narrative of the Ottoman Empire, bearing in mind that the tales of yesteryears are not just echoes of a bygone era but whispers of wisdom for the future. As we turn our gaze to the unfolding chapters of history, we hold the conviction that within these stories lie the keys to comprehending the intricate dance of power, culture, and identity that continues to define our collective journey.

# Interregnum and Restoration

IN THE WAKE OF MURAD I's demise on the fields of Kosovo in 1389, the Ottoman Empire was thrust into a quagmire of chaos—a civil war that would test the very fabric of the burgeoning state. Murad's death left the throne vulnerable, with his sons Bayezid, Yakub, and Savci entangled in a ruthless struggle for power. The ensuing period, known as the Interregnum, was a crucible from which a new order within the empire would emerge.

The central figures of this historical drama were Bayezid and his brothers. Bayezid, the eventual victor, was a seasoned warrior with a vision for the empire that surpassed mere conquest. His brothers, though lesser-known, played significant roles in the power struggle that unfolded. The stage was set for a confrontation that would shape the future trajectory of Ottoman rule.

The core challenge was the absence of a clear succession protocol, which led to the fragmentation of authority and loyalties within the empire. The death of Murad I had left an administrative vacuum that his sons sought to fill, each with his own supporters and military contingents. The result was a brutal and uncompromising civil conflict that put the empire's very existence into question.

Bayezid's approach to resolving this crisis was multifaceted; he combined military prowess with political acumen to overcome his siblings. He first turned his attention to his brother Yakub, securing his elimination through combat. With one adversary out of the way, he then faced Savci, whom he defeated and subsequently showed mercy by sparing his life, a decision that would later come back to haunt him.

The results of Bayezid's strategy were profound. By 1390, he had firmly established himself as the sole ruler of the Ottoman Empire, earning the title Bayezid I. His victory not only ended the civil strife but also led to the restoration of stability within the empire. The way in which Bayezid solidified his reign set a precedent for future Ottoman succession, emphasizing the need for strong, centralized authority to prevent similar episodes of disarray.

Reflecting on this period, it is evident that the Interregnum was both a curse and a blessing for the Ottoman state. It exposed underlying weaknesses in the political structure but also facilitated a period of reform and centralization that would benefit the empire in the long run. Bayezid's triumph was not without criticism; some argued that his ruthless suppression of opposition and centralization of power led to despotism and the curtailment of regional autonomy.

Visual aids like family trees and maps of the empire during the Interregnum would serve to enhance understanding of the complex relationships and territorial divisions that marked this period of Ottoman history.

Bayezid's restoration of stability was significant not only for the Ottoman Empire but also in the broader narrative of empire building. His reign was marked by considerable territorial expansion and the development of administrative institutions that would define Ottoman governance for centuries. The legacy of his rule can be seen as a pivotal moment in the transformation of the empire from a regional power into a formidable force on the world stage.

One must ponder: Could the empire have reached such heights without first enduring the crucible of the Interregnum? The struggle for succession revealed the resilience of Ottoman political structures and the remarkable capability of its leaders to adapt in the face of adversity.

Interregnum and Restoration, therefore, is not just a tale of conflict and resolution but a reflection on the nature of power and the mechanisms of governance. It invites the reader to contemplate the delicate balance between authority and liberty, centralization and division, and the role of individual leadership in shaping the course of history.

As the narrative of 'The Ottoman Empire' progresses, it is imperative to consider how the events of the past continue to resonate in the complexities of modern governance. The story of Bayezid I serves as a profound case study in leadership and statecraft, offering timeless insights into the challenges of succession, the burdens of power, and the ceaseless pursuit of stability in an ever-changing world.

In the next chapter, we delve deeper into the transformative impact of Bayezid's rule. But as we turn the page, let us linger on a question that remains as relevant today as it was centuries ago: How does a leader forge unity in the aftermath of division, and what lessons can we draw from history to guide us in the stewardship of nations?

# Military Innovations

IN THE TURBULENT TAPESTRY of Ottoman history, the empire's military prowess stands out as a thread woven with ingenuity and tenacity. From the shores of the Bosphorus to the gates of Vienna, the Ottoman war machine displayed an array of strategies and innovations that left an indelible mark on the annals of warfare. Among these, the use of the Janissaries and the development of early artillery were pivotal in establishing Ottoman dominance.

But what was it about these military components that gave the Ottomans such a formidable edge? What underlying principles and tactics enabled them to outmaneuver and outfight the armies of Europe and the Middle East?

The Janissaries, an elite infantry corps, were the backbone of the Ottoman army. Initially formed in the 14th century, they evolved into a powerful and disciplined force, one of the first standing armies in Europe since the Roman legions. Their rigorous training and strict hierarchy contrasted with the feudal levies and mercenary bands that made up the armies of their adversaries. Eventually, Janissaries were equipped with muskets and were regularly drilled in their use, setting them above other contemporary militaries.

Artillery, on the other hand, was an area where the Ottomans excelled through innovation. The empire's engineers and foundrymen made significant advances in cannon design and casting, producing guns capable of breaching the strongest walls. The bombardment of Constantinople in 1453, which led to the fall of the city, stands as a testament to the transformative power of Ottoman siege tactics.

Observing these two facets of Ottoman military might, one is drawn to the similarities that underpin their success. Both the Janissaries and the artillery corps were professional units, maintained as permanent fixtures of the empire's military establishment. They were also both beneficiaries of the empire's willingness to adopt and refine new technologies, whether in the crafting of personal firearms or the casting of siege guns.

Yet, the distinctions between them are equally enlightening. The Janissaries, despite their martial focus, were also political players within the empire, wielding significant influence. Their role extended beyond the battlefield, affecting the very governance of the state. Artillery, conversely, was a tool, albeit a revolutionary one, that did not have the same capacity to shape Ottoman policy.

Imagine, if you will, the sight of Janissary troops marching in lockstep, their battalion a sea of uniformity, each soldier a mirror of the other. Now, contrast this with the thunderous roar of cannons, the acrid smoke billowing into the sky as stone walls crumble under the might of Ottoman engineering. These images evoke the dual nature of the empire's military innovations; one an entity of human precision, the other a manifestation of raw power.

What do these comparisons tell us about the broader implications of Ottoman military innovations? They suggest a society that placed great emphasis on organization, discipline, and technological advancement. The empire's success in battle was not merely a product of superior numbers or brute force, but of thoughtful innovation and systemic modernization.

But how do such historical reflections translate to contemporary relevance? Consider the modern military emphasis on special forces, akin to Janissaries in their elite status and rigorous training. Or ponder the ongoing advances in military technology, where the latest developments in artillery during the Ottoman era find their parallels in today's pursuit of cutting-edge weaponry.

Could it be that the lessons of Ottoman military strategy—embracing innovation, maintaining discipline, and valuing professional soldiers—hold enduring truths for the art of war?

As we delve into the nuanced dynamics of early Ottoman military might, one cannot help but pose the question: In what ways do the echoes of Janissary drums and the resonance of cannon fire inform our understanding of military evolution?

Through the lens of history, the story of the Janissaries and Ottoman artillery is not merely an account of conquest and dominance. It is a narrative that speaks to the ingenuity of a civilization and its ability to adapt, innovate, and ultimately, to project power across continents.

In the chapters that follow, we will explore the profound impact these military innovations had on the Ottoman Empire's ascent to greatness. But for now, let us reflect on the realization that the echoes of the past continue to reverberate, reminding us that the art of war is an ever-evolving craft, with each innovation building upon the legacy of those that came before.

# Economic Foundations

AS THE DAWN OF THE Ottoman Empire rose over the horizon, it was not only the clang of swords and the thunder of cannons that heralded its ascendancy. The whispers of silver and the rustle of silk on the trade routes spoke of an emerging power that understood the intricate dance of commerce and economics. The early sultans, those shrewd architects of empire, laid a vast network upon which the pillars of their dominion would rest: the economic foundations that turned a burgeoning state into a formidable empire.

At the heart of the Ottoman economic expanse was a problem, as enduring as it was challenging. The empire sprawled across diverse terrains and cultures, from the rich plains of Anatolia to the spice-scented bazaars of Cairo. How could such a vast and variegated landscape be stitched together into a cohesive economic tapestry?

The consequences of ignoring this quandary were dire. Without a unified economic policy, the empire risked fragmenting under the weight of its own diversity, leaving it vulnerable to external threats and internal strife. The sultans knew that if they failed to integrate the economies of their conquered lands, the empire's glory might be as fleeting as a desert mirage.

The solution lay in a masterful stroke of policy and foresight. The early sultans established robust trade routes and enacted policies that encouraged commerce and craft. They built upon the legacy of the Silk Road, reviving and expanding it to knit together the East and West. The Spice Route, too, became a conduit of wealth, as Ottoman caravans carried precious goods that tantalized the palates and imaginations of Europe.

Implementation of these strategies required both wisdom and wariness. The Ottomans lowered taxes for merchants and provided state protection for caravans. They established standardized weights and measures and minted reliable coinage to facilitate trade. In the maritime realm, the empire's formidable navy patrolled the

Mediterranean, securing the sea lanes against piracy and ensuring the safe passage of goods.

The outcomes of such policies were as bountiful as the fields of the Anatolian heartland. Trade flourished, and with it, the empire's coffers swelled. Markets buzzed with activity as goods from the far reaches of the world exchanged hands. Luxurious textiles, spices, and metals fueled an economic engine that powered the empire's expansion and its military campaigns.

Yet, there were other roads not taken, other solutions that could have shaped the empire's destiny differently. Had the sultans succumbed to the temptation of heavy taxation or isolationism, the story of the Ottoman Empire might have been one of stagnation and decline. But in their wisdom, they chose openness and integration, and the empire thrived.

One can imagine the vibrant lifeblood of the empire's economy pulsing through its trade routes. Picture, if you will, the bazaars, where the air is thick with the scent of incense and the murmur of a thousand tongues bartering, a kaleidoscope of color from the wares on display. Can you see the caravans, laden with goods, winding their way across the landscape like the veins of a great being, connecting organ to organ, city to city?

This is the empire in motion, a living entity sustained by the flow of commerce.

But what of today? What lessons can the modern world glean from the economic strategies of the early Ottomans? Perhaps it is the recognition that trade is an engine of prosperity and a bridge between civilizations. Maybe it is an understanding that diversity can be a strength, not a weakness, when woven together with the threads of economic policy and mutual benefit.

Ask yourself: How often do we consider the impact of economic integration on the stability of a nation? Do we fully grasp the potential of commerce to unite disparate peoples and regions?

The economic foundations laid by the early Ottoman sultans were not merely about wealth. They were about creating a resilient structure that could support the weight of an empire. As we continue to explore the complex tapestry of Ottoman history, let us not forget that beneath the martial triumphs and the grandeur of palaces, it was the silent strength of trade routes and economic policies that helped to forge an empire that stood the test of time.

# Age of Expansion

## Conquering Constantinople

Few events hold as much gravitas as the siege and fall of Constantinople. Known as the "Queen of Cities," this majestic metropolis was the heart of the Byzantine Empire, a beacon of Christian civilization and a testament to the enduring legacy of Rome. Its formidable walls had thwarted invaders for over a millennium, but in 1453, fate would cast a shadow over the city's hallowed ramparts.

What ancient prophecy could have foreseen the day when the crescent would rise above the cross in the storied capital of Byzantium? The tale of Constantinople's fall is one of audacious strategy, towering ambition, and the relentless march of an empire seeking its place in the annals of history.

Long before the Ottomans set their sights on the city, Constantinople had been the jewel of emperors. Founded by Constantine the Great in 330 AD on the site of ancient Byzantium, the city was envisioned as a "New Rome." Its strategic location straddled Europe and Asia, and its wealth and splendor became the envy of the world.

Through the centuries, the city encountered numerous sieges. The Avars, Arabs, Rus', Bulgarians, and Crusaders all hungered for its riches, yet none could penetrate its mighty Theodosian Walls. It was not until the Fourth Crusade in 1204 that the city was brutally sacked, not by a foreign enemy, but by fellow Christians. Though the Byzantines would later reclaim and restore their capital, the empire was left a shadow of its former self, setting the stage for its ultimate demise.

The story of the Ottoman ascension is one of relentless expansion. From their origins as a small principality in the late 13th century, the Ottomans grew to become a powerful force in the region, conquering much of the Balkans and steadily chipping away at Byzantine territory. Key milestones in their march towards empire included the Battle of Bapheus in 1302, the capture of Bursa in 1326, which became the Ottoman capital, and the victory at the Battle of Kosovo in 1389, which paved the way for further incursions into Europe.

By the time Sultan Mehmed II, known as Mehmed the Conqueror, ascended the Ottoman throne in 1451, the conquest of Constantinople was not a question of "if" but "when." His predecessors had dreamt of it, but Mehmed was determined to turn dreams into decisive action.

Imagine, if you will, the formidable sight that met the eyes of Constantinople's defenders in the spring of 1453. The horizon teemed with a sea of Ottoman tents, the air thrummed with the anticipation of battle, and the waters of the Golden Horn swarmed with a navy eager to breach the city's defenses. Mehmed had amassed a force rumored to be upwards of 100,000 men, accompanied by a fleet of 126 ships. Against them stood the beleaguered city, guarded by a garrison of merely 7,000 to 10,000 soldiers, beseeching the heavens for deliverance.

The siege that ensued was not merely a military assault; it was a clash of civilizations. For 53 days, the city withstood the relentless Ottoman bombardment. Massive cannons, the likes of which the world had never seen, designed by the Hungarian engineer Orban, hurled stone balls weighing over half a ton against the ancient Theodosian Walls. Yet, the defenders, led by the valiant Emperor Constantine XI Palaiologos and an array of foreign soldiers, including the fabled Genoese mercenary Giovanni Giustiniani, held fast.

How could the world have remained silent as the last remnant of Rome gasped for breath? Yet, help was scant and hope dimmed with each passing day. The Byzantines had long possessed the secret of Greek fire, a fearsome weapon that once repelled Arab fleets. But no weapon could withstand the tide of history, and on the fateful morning of May 29, 1453, the city's fate was sealed. The Ottomans breached the walls at the St. Romanus Gate, and a frenzied melee ensued. The emperor, whose body was never found, was said to have fallen in battle, his last words lost to the clamor of a dying empire.

The conquest of Constantinople was not merely a military victory; it was a transformative moment that reshaped the region's cultural tapestry. The Ottomans were quick to establish their dominion, converting the magnificent Hagia Sophia into a mosque and setting about the creation of a new Islamic capital that would draw scholars, artists, and merchants from across the world. The city, now known as Istanbul, would flourish under Ottoman rule, becoming a nexus of trade and culture that bridged East and West.

What lessons do we glean from the fall of Constantinople? The city's legacy is a mosaic of human endeavor, resilience, and the inexorable tide of change. Today, Istanbul stands as a vibrant metropolis, a place where the echoes of the past are still heard amidst the bustle of modern life. The fall of Constantinople marked the end of one era, but it also heralded the dawn of another, a chapter written by those who dared to dream and conquer.

In the shadow of the city's ancient walls, one may ponder the whims of fate. What if the Byzantine pleas for help had stirred Christendom into action? What if the city had withstood Mehmed's siege? History, however, is not crafted by what-ifs, but by the resolute actions of those who shape it. The Ottoman Empire rose on the ashes of Byzantium, and the world would never be the same. How will the stories of today's empires be recounted by the scribes of the future? Only time will tell.

# Suleiman the Magnificent

AS THE DUST SETTLED on the shattered remnants of the Byzantine Empire, a new era dawned upon the crossroads of the world. The once indomitable walls of Constantinople, now bearing the scars of siege and conquest, looked upon an empire eager to carve its name into the annals of history. Out of the ashes of conquest rose a phoenix that would extend its wings over lands far beyond the horizon. This phoenix, the Ottoman Empire, would reach the zenith of its power under the rule of a sultan whose name would echo through the corridors of time: Suleiman the Magnificent.

Turn your gaze to the early 16th century, a time when Europe was fragmented, grappling with the throes of religious reformation and political strife. To the East, vast empires like the Safavids in Persia simmered with latent rivalry. It was within this crucible of power and ambition that Suleiman ascended the Ottoman throne in 1520, at the tender age of 26. His inheritance? An empire at the cusp of greatness, yearning for a leader with the vision and strength to guide it to its apex.

What forces of destiny propelled the son of Selim the Grim to such monumental heights? Suleiman's reign was marked by a series of conquests that would not only expand the empire's boundaries but also its cultural and political influence. With each campaign, whether it was the siege of Rhodes in 1522, the conquest of Belgrade in 1521, or the victory at the Battle of Mohács in 1526, which left the Kingdom of Hungary in tatters, Suleiman's legend grew. His fleets commanded the Mediterranean, and his armies threatened the gates of Vienna, sending shivers down the spine of Christendom.

Yet, can the measure of a ruler be taken solely by the lands they conquer? Suleiman's legacy was not wrought by the sword alone. His rule heralded an era of unparalleled prosperity and cultural efflorescence, known as the Ottoman Golden Age. Do you not wonder how the legal and administrative reforms he instituted, known as the "Suleimanic Legisprudence," reshaped an empire?

Suleiman's laws, the Kanun, were a beacon of justice that streamlined governance and facilitated the integration of diverse peoples under the Ottoman banner. His court, under the stewardship of the wise Grand Vizier Pargalı Ibrahim Pasha, became a crucible for talent, attracting scholars, poets, and artists from across the known world. How could one not marvel at the architectural splendor of the Süleymaniye Mosque, a testament to the genius of the imperial architect Mimar Sinan?

In the intricate patterns of Iznik tiles, the lilting strains of Ottoman court music, and the vibrant energy of Istanbul's bazaars, one can still perceive the echoes of Suleiman's vision. His patronage of the arts and education sowed the seeds for a cultural renaissance that would enrich the tapestry of human history. Can you fathom the impact of a ruler who not only wields absolute power but also possesses a poet's soul, writing under the nom de plume Muhibbi?

Why, then, does the reign of Suleiman the Magnificent matter in the world of today? In an age where the clash of ideologies and the strife for cultural identity dominate the global discourse, Suleiman's empire stands as a reminder of a time when a melting pot of cultures thrived under a single ruler. His ability to balance power with justice, war with peace, and ambition with wisdom offers a lens through which one might examine the complexities of modern governance and coexistence.

As we stand witness to the rise and fall of nations in our own time, are we not compelled to reflect on the enduring lessons from Suleiman's rule? How do we harness the spirit of tolerance and innovation that marked his era to address the challenges of our own? How do we reconcile the pursuit of power with the imperative to forge a legacy of enduring peace and prosperity?

Let us, then, journey through the pages of history to unravel the story of Suleiman the Magnificent. His was a life draped in the tapestry of power, woven with threads of gold and shadow. As you delve into the following chapters, prepare to be transported to a world where the whispers of the past breathe life into the present, and the drumbeat of an empire's heart reverberates through the ages.

Suleiman's reign stands as an indelible marker, not just in the chronicles of the Ottoman Empire, but in the grand narrative of human civilization. Its study is not an idle pursuit of bygone glories, but a venture of understanding that lights the path forward. What, then, shall we learn from the sultan who gazed upon the world from his throne in Istanbul and saw not limits, but possibilities?

## Naval Supremacy in the Mediterranean

THROUGHOUT MARITIME history, few tales capture the imagination quite like the Ottoman dominance over the Mediterranean Sea. It was a time when the whisper of sails and the roar of cannons echoed across the waters, heralding an era when control of trade and power was asserted not by land, but by sea. At the heart of this dominance lay a series of confrontations that pitted the burgeoning Ottoman navy against the seasoned maritime forces of Europe. Among these, the Battle of Preveza stands as a paramount example of Ottoman naval strategy and its implications on the balance of power in the Mediterranean.

Imagine the Mediterranean of the 16th century, a sprawling expanse of blue that served as the stage for an epic struggle for supremacy. The Ottoman Empire, having secured its hold on the former Byzantine territories, was keenly aware that true control of its empire hinged on its ability to dominate these waters. European powers, equally cognizant of this fact, were not about to relinquish their maritime heritage or their profitable trade routes without a fight. This was the backdrop against which the Battle of Preveza would unfold.

Enter the main players: on one side, the indomitable Ottoman fleet, commanded by the legendary admiral Hayreddin Barbarossa. His very name struck fear into the hearts of sailors across the Mediterranean. On the opposing side, the Holy League, a formidable alliance of European naval powers led by the Republic of Venice and supported by the Papacy, Spain, and others, under the command of the Genoese admiral Andrea Doria. These were seasoned powers, each with a storied history on the high seas, now converging in a clash that would echo through history.

The challenge was clear: the Holy League sought to break the Ottoman stranglehold on the Mediterranean trade routes and reaffirm Christian dominance. The Ottomans, meanwhile, aimed to cement their control and secure their empire's economic lifeline.

How did Barbarossa approach this monumental challenge? His strategy was one of preemptive audacity and meticulous preparation. Barbarossa consolidated his forces at the strategically crucial port of Preveza, fortifying his position and securing the support of local forces. With the bay's narrow entrance and the fort's guns covering the channel, the Ottomans had a natural advantage.

As the Holy League fleet approached, the battle lines were drawn. Barbarossa's fleet, composed of galleys and galliots, was outnumbered but not outmaneuvered. He employed a defensive crescent formation, forcing Doria's galleons to engage in the confined waters, where their size became a disadvantage.

The result was a decisive Ottoman victory. Barbarossa's skillful maneuvering and the effective use of the fort's artillery decimated the Holy League fleet. The Battle of Preveza not only solidified Ottoman control over the Eastern Mediterranean but also showcased their naval prowess to the world.

Reflecting on this engagement, one cannot help but be struck by the foresight and strategic acumen displayed by the Ottoman command. The victory at Preveza was not merely a triumph of numbers or firepower, but of tactical brilliance and a deep understanding of the maritime chessboard.

This event, while a single chapter in the broader narrative of the Ottoman Empire's history, encapsulates the pivotal role that naval power played in shaping the geopolitical contours of the Mediterranean. The waves that washed over the decks of Barbarossa's galleys carried with them the future of empires and the fate of nations.

And what of the wider implications? The Ottoman dominance at sea during this period underlines a crucial theme in the empire's overarching story: the fusion of military might with commercial acumen. It was this combination that allowed the Ottomans to control the sinews of trade and influence that crisscrossed the Mediterranean basin.

As we contemplate the echoes of cannon fire over Preveza, a question lingers: How does the contest for control of a sea mirror the broader human struggle for power and influence? The Ottoman mastery of the Mediterranean is a testament to the enduring truth that the arteries of commerce and the veins of military power are often one and the same.

# The European Frontier

AS THE DAWN LIGHT CREPT across the European landscape, it illuminated an empire on the cusp of a remarkable transformation. The Ottoman Empire, a burgeoning power that had already left an indelible mark upon the Mediterranean, now turned its gaze toward the rich and fragmented tapestry of Europe. The push into this new frontier was not merely a campaign for more land; it was a quest to etch the Ottoman name into the annals of a continent that had long been the cradle of great empires.

What drove this formidable force to venture beyond their well-established domains in Asia Minor and the Levant? What were the implications of their relentless march towards the heart of Europe? These questions guide our exploration into one of the most pivotal eras of the Ottoman expansion—their advance into European territories, culminating in the significant Battle of Mohacs and the subsequent sieges that brought the Ottomans to the gates of Vienna.

The Ottomans, under the rule of Suleiman the Magnificent, sought not just to conquer but to integrate the mosaic of European realms into their diverse empire. The claim was clear: Europe presented an opportunity to extend the Ottoman influence, control critical trade routes, and secure strategic positions against European adversaries.

The primary evidence of this claim lies in the Battle of Mohacs, fought on the 29th of August 1526. This battle, a clash between the forces of the Ottoman Empire and the Kingdom of Hungary, was more than a military engagement; it was a statement of intent. It showcased the might of the Ottoman war machine and underscored the empire's ability to project power far from its traditional strongholds.

Delving deeper, the battle was marked by the use of superior tactics and the presence of artillery, which the Ottomans employed with devastating effect. The Hungarian army, led by the young King Louis II, was ill-prepared to face the disciplined Ottoman forces. The result was a catastrophic defeat for Hungary, leading to the death of their king and the destabilization of their kingdom. The Ottomans emerged victorious, their path to further European incursions now wide open.

Yet, there are counterarguments to consider. Some historians argue that the significance of Mohacs has been overstated, suggesting that it was but one of many battles and that it was the failure of European powers to effectively unite against the Ottoman threat that truly shaped the course of history.

In rebuttal, while unity among European states was indeed lacking, it would be a disservice to diminish the strategic acumen demonstrated by the Ottomans at Mohacs. The battle had profound consequences, leading to the partition of Hungary and the eventual establishment of the Ottoman province of Budin.

Additional supporting evidence of the Ottoman advance into Europe is found in their sieges of Vienna in 1529 and again in 1683.

These sieges, although ultimately unsuccessful, speak volumes about the extent of Ottoman ambition and the fear they instilled in the heart of Europe. The very notion of Ottoman troops at the doorstep of Vienna sent shockwaves through European courts, prompting alliances that would have been previously unthinkable.

In conclusion, the Ottoman expansion into Europe, epitomized by the Battle of Mohacs and the push towards Vienna, was a transformative period that reshaped the continent's political and cultural landscape. The Ottomans, by venturing into Europe, challenged the established order and left a legacy that is still palpable in the cultural and religious tapestry of modern Europe. Their ambition and military prowess during this era serve as a testament to their role as a formidable force that shaped the destiny of a continent.

## The East and the Safavids

IN THE CHRONICLES OF history, few rivalries have been as intense or as impactful as that between the Ottoman Empire and the Safavid Empire. This chapter delves into the intricacies of their relationship, a tapestry woven with threads of fervent ideology and the pursuit of dominance. Bearing witness to their complex interactions is the pivotal Battle of Chaldiran, a conflict that not only shaped the destiny of these empires but also the geopolitical contours of the Middle East.

The Ottoman Empire, a Sunni colossus, and the Safavid Empire, a bastion of Shia Islam, were more than mere neighbors. They were ideological adversaries, each intent on expanding its influence and religious doctrine. The significance of their conflict transcends mere territorial disputes; it was a battle for the soul of Islam and the hegemony of the region.

Why compare these two empires, one might ask? It is through such a comparison that the undercurrents of 16th-century politics, culture, and religion become evident, offering us a glimpse into the broader implications of their strife.

The criteria for our analysis are multifaceted. We consider military prowess, leadership, religious fervor, and statecraft. These benchmarks are critical to understanding the profound impact of the Ottoman-Safavid rivalry.

In a balanced view, we see similarities between these empires in their imperial ambitions and their use of military innovations. Both the Ottomans and the Safavids were adept at incorporating gunpowder technology into their arsenals, revolutionizing warfare in the Islamic world. Furthermore, they shared a penchant for architectural grandeur, as evidenced by the splendid mosques and palaces that dotted their capitals, Istanbul and Isfahan.

Yet the distinctions are stark and telling. The Sunnism of the Ottomans was grounded in the established orthodoxies of the Caliphate's legacy, while the Safavids championed Shia Islam, a sect that had faced marginalization for centuries. This religious divide was not merely theological; it was a schism that manifested in their governance, legal systems, and societal norms.

Visual aids are not present in this text, yet one can imagine the vivid contrasts if they were to be depicted: the sun setting over Istanbul's skyline, silhouetting minarets against a crimson sky, while in Isfahan, the intricate blue tiles of the mosques reflect the morning light, symbolizing the dichotomy of two empires under the same sun yet worlds apart.

The Battle of Chaldiran, fought on August 23, 1514, showcases the zenith of this rivalry. The Ottoman forces, led by Sultan Selim I, faced the Safavids under Shah Ismail I in a clash that was as much about military might as it was about proving the supremacy of one sect over the other. The Ottomans, with their superior organization and use of artillery, dealt a severe blow to the Safavid troops, who were formidable but less familiar with modern warfare tactics.

What does this reveal? The outcome at Chaldiran underscored the importance of technological adaptability in warfare and highlighted the peril of religious zeal clouding strategic judgment. The Safavids' belief in the divine support for their cause may have emboldened their spirit, but it did little to protect them from the cannons of the Ottomans.

While the battle did not end the Safavid dynasty, it significantly curtailed its expansion westward and cemented the Ottoman dominance in the region. The broader implications are profound. The frontier between the two empires became a lasting demarcation between Sunni and Shia Islam, a divide that echoes through the centuries to the present day.

In our contemporary world, the legacy of this historic rivalry is palpable. The modern Middle East, with its complex tapestry of sectarian conflicts, can trace some of its origins to the Ottoman-Safavid divide. The Battle of Chaldiran, therefore, is not just a historical footnote; it is a chapter that continues to influence the narrative of a region that remains a fulcrum of global politics.

In conclusion, the examination of the Ottoman and Safavid empires, particularly through the lens of the Battle of Chaldiran, offers more than a mere recounting of history. It presents a saga of two powers locked in a struggle that shaped the course of an era. The echoes of their cannons might have long since faded, but the reverberations of their conflict continue to inform the present, a testament to their enduring impact on the world stage. Through this exploration, we gain not only a deeper understanding of the past but also insights that illuminate the complexities of the present.

# Golden Age

## Architectural Marvels

The skyline of Istanbul, punctuated by its majestic minarets and grand domes, tells a story of the Ottoman Empire's former glory—a narrative etched in stone and marble across centuries. Within this tableau, certain structures stand as testaments to Ottoman ingenuity and splendor. Among them, the Suleymaniye Mosque and Topkapi Palace are paragons that demand exploration to appreciate their historical and cultural significance fully.

In anticipation of the history about to unfold on the pages before us, let us first enumerate the architectural treasures that will be the focus of our in-depth journey. The Suleymaniye Mosque, a harmonious blend of spirituality and grandeur, will be our starting point. Following this, we shall traverse the opulent chambers of Topkapi Palace, a symbol of imperial power. Each edifice, with its unique narrative, offers a window into the Ottoman world.

## SULEYMANIYE MOSQUE

THE SULEYMANIYE MOSQUE, a magnificent creation of the famed architect Mimar Sinan, stands as a crowning achievement of Ottoman architecture. Commissioned by Sultan Suleiman the Magnificent in the 16th century, its construction was an endeavor of both ambition and devotion. Could the stones of its walls speak, they would tell tales of a sultan's desire to inscribe his faith in the skyline of his capital.

Sinan, a master of his craft, engineered a complex that transcended the mere function of a place of worship. The mosque's central dome, soaring 53 meters high, appears to defy gravity. Four slender minarets, each with ten balconies, signify Suleiman's status as the fourth sultan after the establishment of the Ottoman caliphate.

Historians and travelers alike have been enthralled by the mosque's synthesis of space and light. Sinan himself regarded the Suleymaniye as his masterpiece, a work that embodied his principles of balance and proportion. The interior, illuminated by an array of 138 windows, is a tapestry of intricate Iznik tiles.

The practical applications of the mosque's design are equally noteworthy. The complex included a hospital, a kitchen for the poor, a caravanserai, and a bathhouse—each element serving the community and ensuring the mosque's place at the heart of Ottoman social life.

## TOPKAPI PALACE

TRANSITIONING FROM the religious to the imperial, we turn our gaze to Topkapi Palace, the epicenter of Ottoman power for nearly four centuries. Envisioned by Sultan Mehmed II after his conquest of Constantinople, the palace was more than a private residence; it was a microcosm of the empire, encapsulating its might, culture, and administration.

With its labyrinthine arrangement of courtyards, chambers, and pavilions, Topkapi Palace unfolds like a tale of intrigue and opulence. The Imperial Council Chamber, with its conical dome and ornate decorations, was where state affairs were deliberated. The Harem, a secluded world within a world, was the private domain of the sultan and his family, guarded by the eunuchs and shrouded in mystery.

The treasury of Topkapi bears witness to the empire's wealth, housing jewels and artifacts of untold value. Among these treasures, the Topkapi Dagger and the Spoonmaker's Diamond are stuff of legend, emblematic of the empire's reach and the spoils of conquest.

The palace not only served as the heart of the empire but also as an engine of cultural patronage. It supported artisans, poets, and scholars, thereby fostering an environment where the arts and sciences could flourish. Today, as a museum, Topkapi continues to educate and inspire, its legacy undiminished by the passage of time.

In the annals of history, the Suleymaniye Mosque and Topkapi Palace are more than mere buildings; they are enduring chronicles of human endeavor. They stand as reminders of what was once the center of a vast and powerful empire, their architectural beauty and complexity captivating the imaginations of those who walk their corridors today. Have you, dear reader, ever considered the hands that carved their intricate designs, or the countless footsteps that have crossed their thresholds?

In the grand narrative of the Ottoman Empire, these marvels are chapters that resonate with the echoes of the past. As the sunlight plays upon their surfaces and their shadows dance upon the ground, we are reminded of the empire's enduring legacy—a legacy that continues to speak to us through the language of its stones.

# The Ottoman Renaissance

THE EMBERS OF CREATIVITY and intellectual fervor were always simmering within the Ottoman Empire, but it was during the 16th century that they burst into a magnificent flame—a period that would come to be known as the Ottoman Renaissance. This era, ripe with artistic and scholarly advancements, beckoned a wave of cultural revival and innovation that paralleled the grandeur of its European counterpart.

At the heart of this renaissance was a confluence of diverse influences, from Persian and Arab lands to the farthest reaches of Europe. The Ottoman court, with its insatiable appetite for knowledge and beauty, became the crucible where these varied elements melded to forge something truly transcendent.

The polymath and literary genius Matrakci Nasuh embodies the spirit of this age. A master of many disciplines, his works spanned mathematics, swordsmanship, and the visual arts. His "miniature" paintings, brimming with vibrant colors and meticulous detail, offered a window into the Ottoman world, from the bustling streets of Istanbul to the verdant landscapes of newly conquered territories.

Another luminary was the poet Baki, known as the Sultan of Poets. His lyrical mastery in divan poetry—a form characterized by its intricate rhyming patterns and metaphorical language—captured the complexity of human emotions and the splendor of the court. His magnum opus, "The Elegy for Sultan Suleiman," remains a poignant epitome of Ottoman literature, as it laments the passing of an era under Suleiman the Magnificent.

What of the scholars, you might inquire, who toiled away in the pursuit of knowledge? Figures like Takiyüddin al-Rasid, who, with the patronage of Murad III, established an observatory in Istanbul rivaling that of Tycho Brahe's Uraniborg. His astronomical tables and instruments were not merely scientific tools but also works of art, adorned with intricate calligraphy and celestial motifs.

In the realm of architecture, the Ottoman Renaissance saw a harmonization of various styles, synthesizing Byzantine, Persian, and Islamic elements. The genius of Mimar Sinan continued to unfold in structures like the Şehzade Mosque and the Mihrimah Sultan Mosque, where the interplay of light and dome created an ethereal ambiance.

Amidst these artistic and intellectual pursuits, the influence of the printing press began to take hold. Though initially met with resistance, this technological marvel eventually found its place in the empire, broadening the dissemination of knowledge and ideas.

One cannot ignore the role of women in this cultural flowering. Hürrem Sultan, also known as Roxelana, was not only the influential consort of Suleiman the Magnificent but also a patron of the arts, commissioning works and supporting charitable institutions. Her impact on the empire's cultural landscape was indelible, proving that the renaissance was not solely the domain of men.

To gaze upon the works born of this era is to behold a tapestry woven from threads of innovation and tradition. Each painting, poem, and edifice resonates with a sense of identity that was uniquely Ottoman, yet attuned to the broader currents of the world.

As we reflect upon this remarkable period, a question lingers in the air: What can we learn from the Ottoman Renaissance today? Perhaps it is a reminder of the transformative power of cultural exchange, the importance of supporting the arts, and the enduring legacy of intellectual curiosity.

In closing, the Ottoman Renaissance was not just a historical epoch—it was a testament to human creativity and the unyielding quest for knowledge. The key takeaways from this chapter in Ottoman history are the value of interdisciplinary pursuits, the impact of patronage in the arts, and the unending potential of cross-cultural interaction. These lessons, as vibrant and relevant as the era they hail from, continue to inspire and guide us in our own quests for enlightenment.

## Ottoman Law and Administration

THE OTTOMAN EMPIRE, a vast and complex realm, stood as a testament to the power of effective governance. Its ability to maintain control over diverse territories was in no small part due to its sophisticated legal reforms and administrative organization. This chapter delves into the depths of the empire's bureaucratic mechanisms and legal frameworks that were the sinews and bones of its body politic.

Embarking on this journey, one's objective is clear: to understand the intricacies of the Ottoman legal and administrative systems that allowed for unified rule across a mosaic of cultures and religions.

To comprehend the empire's administrative prowess, one must first grasp the prerequisites that laid its foundation. These were the Islamic legal tradition, the well-established Turkish practices of governance, and the pragmatic adaptations of existing systems from conquered lands.

Imagine a canvas painted with broad strokes that outline the empire's governance: at the top, the Sultan, the absolute ruler whose word was law; beneath him, the Imperial Council, assisting in state matters; and further down, a hierarchy of officials, each with their own roles in the intricate machinery of state.

Now, let us paint with finer detail, starting with the legal system, which was primarily derived from Islamic law, or Sharia. However, the Ottomans did not apply Sharia in isolation. They intertwined it with the "kanuns," or sultanic laws, which addressed the administrative and fiscal needs of the state. The blending of religious and secular laws enabled the empire to cater to a multifaceted society while maintaining religious legitimacy.

What of the administrative divisions? The empire was divided into provinces, or "vilayets," managed by governors, or "wālīs," who reported directly to the Sultan. Each vilayet was further segmented into districts, "sanjaks," overseen by "sanjakbeys," and then into smaller units, "kazas," each administered by a "kadi," or judge. This hierarchical structure facilitated central control, yet allowed for local autonomy—a delicate balance that was key to the empire's longevity.

Amidst this complexity, practical advice for officials was abundant. Manuals like the "Kanunnames" provided guidelines on governance, stressing the importance of justice, fiscal responsibility, and the welfare of the people. Could it be that the success of the Ottoman administration lay in these very texts?

To verify the effectiveness of this system, one need only look at the longevity of the Ottoman rule and its ability to integrate diverse peoples. The empire's legal and administrative reforms were continually tested and refined through centuries of expansion and challenge.

However, no system is without flaws. Troubleshooting was an ongoing task for the Ottomans, with issues such as corruption, local rebellions, and the occasional misuse of power. The solutions often involved revising laws, restructuring administrative units, or even deposing unscrupulous officials.

What then, dear reader, can we glean from the Ottoman's approach to law and administration? Is it not a marvel how they spun the threads of legality and bureaucracy into a tapestry that held together an empire spanning three continents?

Let us pause for a moment. Have you ever considered the monumental task of managing such a diverse empire? It was a constant balancing act, a dance of precision and adaptability. The Ottomans were masters of this dance, their steps guided by the music of pragmatism and tradition.

The Ottoman legal and administrative systems stand as a powerful legacy of governance. The empire's ability to adapt and integrate various legal traditions under one umbrella is a testament to its sophisticated understanding of rule and management. It is a story that speaks volumes about the art of governance, a narrative that continues to resonate in the annals of history.

As the sun set on the Ottoman Empire, its shadows cast long into the future, touching upon modern concepts of statecraft and administration.

# Trade and Prosperity

WITHIN THE BUSTLING markets of Istanbul, amidst the fragrant stalls of spices and the vibrant tapestries of silk, the heart of the Ottoman Empire's economic prowess beat with fervent intensity. This realm, bridging East and West, was a central hub of commerce where the Silk Road converged with the spice trade, weaving a rich tapestry of cultural and economic exchange. It was a place where caravans and ships alike deposited their treasures from afar, and from whence the empire's own goods ventured forth to distant lands.

The main players in this grand bazaar of exchange were not just the merchants and the traders, but also the state officials and the Sultan himself, who recognized the importance of trade and actively worked to promote and protect it. These individuals were the architects of prosperity, ensuring that the economic arteries of the empire remained open and vibrant.

The challenge was manifold: to maintain a secure environment for trade, to manage the flow of goods, and to capitalize on the empire's strategic position. The Ottoman authorities had to navigate through a complex network of trade routes and political alliances, safeguarding their interests while fostering an environment conducive to economic growth.

The solution lay in a series of strategic moves. The Ottomans granted trading privileges and protection to foreign merchants, fostered the development of caravanserais - inns for merchants and their caravans - and invested in a formidable navy to protect their shipping lanes. They understood that prosperity came not from isolation, but from the vibrant exchange of goods, ideas, and culture.

The results were nothing short of remarkable. Istanbul, the empire's crown jewel, flourished into one of the world's wealthiest cities, a testament to the success of these strategies. The empire's coffers swelled with revenues from customs duties and taxes on goods. The prosperity was not limited to the capital; it spread throughout the provinces, where local markets thrived under the umbrella of the empire's economic stability.

Critical reflection on this period reveals that while the Ottoman approach to trade was largely successful, it was not immune to challenges. The reliance on trade meant that disruptions, whether due to war or shifts in trade routes, could have significant consequences. Yet, the overall adaptability and shrewd economic policies of the Ottomans ensured that such disruptions were often temporary and that recovery was swift.

Visual aids depicting the bustling markets, the extensive trade routes, and the grandeur of the caravanserais would serve to bring this historical epoch to life, enabling a more tangible grasp of the empire's commercial vibrancy.

This case study of trade within the Ottoman Empire connects back to the larger narrative of how commerce was a cornerstone of its success. The empire's strategic geographic position was not merely a political asset but a commercial boon, one that allowed it to become a nexus of global trade routes.

One must wonder, what if the winds of change had blown differently? What if the Silk Road had diminished in importance earlier, or the spice trade had been rerouted? These questions linger in the mind, prompting further contemplation of the delicate interplay between geography, politics, and economics.

Trade and prosperity within the Ottoman Empire were not simply about the exchange of goods; they were about the exchange of cultures, knowledge, and ideas. They were about the empire's ability to harness its geographic destiny and weave it into a legacy of wealth and cultural richness. As the pages of history turn, the empire's narrative of trade continues to echo through time, reminding us of the enduring power of economic foresight and strategic positioning.

# Cultural Synthesis

THE OTTOMAN EMPIRE, an enduring note in human history, was more than a political entity; it was a crucible of cultural fusion. Here, in this mosaic of civilization, myriad customs, languages, and beliefs melded together under the aegis of imperial governance, creating a legacy as opulent and diverse as the empire's borders.

To understand this phenomenon, one must first grasp the concept of cultural synthesis. Simply put, it is the process by which different cultures come together to form a new, cohesive whole. As elements from each culture intermingle and influence one another, a new hybrid culture emerges, characterized by shared traditions, practices, and knowledge.

The Ottoman Empire exemplified cultural synthesis in its most resplendent form. At its zenith, it spanned three continents, enveloping the sophisticated Byzantine Empire, the Arab heartlands, and the rustic expanses of the Balkans and Caucasus. Each region, each city, each community contributed threads to the empire's cultural fabric.

The key elements of this synthesis were manifold. Language, for instance, evolved within the empire's borders. Turkish, the lingua franca, absorbed Persian and Arabic vocabulary, while Ottoman Turkish itself became a literary and administrative language rich in complexity and expression.

The historical context of the empire's formation lends insight into its cultural richness. Founded at the close of the thirteenth century, the Ottomans inherited the remnants of the Roman and Byzantine empires, along with the Seljuk Turkish traditions. The Ottomans, adept at administration and warfare, also proved to be connoisseurs of culture, assimilating and adapting the customs of the lands they conquered.

When one situates the Ottoman experience within a broader framework, it becomes clear that the empire was a bridge between East and West. It not only centralized the trade routes that connected Asia and Europe but also facilitated the exchange of ideas and art.

Illustrative examples of cultural synthesis are found in the empire's culinary traditions, where the rich stews of Central Asia met the spices of the Middle East and the fresh ingredients of the Mediterranean. Similarly, music and dance forms blended Central Asian, Arab, and Balkan influences, creating unique genres that continue to enchant audiences today.

However, common misconceptions often oversimplify the Ottoman Empire's cultural legacy. In reality, the empire's culture was a nuanced and vibrant pastiche, shaped by the contributions of Armenians, Greeks, Arabs, Kurds, and many others.

The Ottoman Empire's cultural synthesis is not just a historical curiosity; it has left indelible marks on the modern world. The Balkans, the Middle East, and North Africa still reflect the empire's influence in their languages, their cuisine, and their architecture.

With every stroke of the brush, every note of music, every word penned in the flowing Ottoman script, the empire's subjects celebrated the synthesis of their cultures. It was in these expressions of art and daily life that the true essence of the Ottoman cultural legacy was found – not overshadowed by the might of empires and wars, but shining in the shared humanity of its people.

Thus, as the sun set on the Ottoman Empire, it left behind a cultural legacy that transcends time, a testament to human creativity and resilience.

# Stagnation and Reform

## The Loss of Military Edge

In the fading light of a once-glorious empire, the Ottoman military, an institution that had instilled fear across continents and had dictated the course of history, found itself grappling with a formidable tide of change. As the sun dipped below the horizon on countless battlefields, it became increasingly evident that the strength and tactics that had once secured dominance were now relics of a bygone era.

The Ottoman Empire's military machine had been the architect of many a victory, carving out an empire that spanned three continents. However, the formidable force that had once marched triumphantly through the gates of Constantinople was now facing an existential threat, not from an external enemy, but from the rust of stagnation and the relentless march of progress elsewhere.

The winds of change were howling, carrying with them the sounds of industrial revolution and military innovation from the heart of Europe. The Ottoman's reliance on traditional methods of warfare, once the spine of their military prowess, had become their Achilles' heel.

Should this imbalance persist, the consequences were clear: the empire would be outmaneuvered, outgunned, and potentially carved up by its more technologically advanced and strategically agile European neighbors. The very survival of the Ottoman state was at stake.

The solution, however, was as daunting as the problem itself. Modernization was the clarion call – a thorough and systemic transformation of the military from the ground up. This entailed not just the procurement of modern armaments, but a complete overhaul of military doctrine, training regimes, and command structures.

Implementing such sweeping reforms would require a steadfast commitment from the highest echelons of the Ottoman hierarchy. It would begin with an extensive study of European military systems, followed by the establishment of military academies modeled after those in the West. Advisors and experts from progressive nations would be sought, and young Ottoman officers would be sent abroad to learn and bring back the knowledge that could seed change.

Evidence of the potential success of such reforms could be found by looking at the Meiji Restoration in Japan, which demonstrated how an Eastern power could rapidly modernize its military and compete on the world stage. The Ottoman Empire, likewise, could seek inspiration from the Japanese model, adapting it to the unique cultural and historical context of their own nation.

However, modernization was not the only path that could be taken. An alternative solution, one steeped in the pride of traditional warfare, suggested a different approach: a return to the core principles that had once made the Ottoman military great. This school of thought advocated for a revival of the warrior ethos, rigorous discipline, and the use of elite forces like the Janissaries. Yet, such nostalgic reverie risked ignoring the undeniable advancements of the time and could lead to further isolation and defeat.

In the grand chambers of the empire's decision-makers, the debate raged on. To choose modernization was to embrace uncertainty and the challenge of change. To cling to tradition was to hold onto an identity that was deeply woven into the fabric of the empire. The choice was stark, the stakes were high, and the clock was unrelenting in its tick towards the future.

But what if the empire chose wrongly? What if the path of modernization led to a loss of identity, or worse, a failure to catch up to the European powers? And what if the romanticized past, once revived, proved impotent against the realities of modern conflict?

As the reader reflects on these questions, they are drawn into the narrative, into the very heart of the empire's quandary. With each turn of the page, the weight of history presses down, the urgency of the decision pulses with the rhythm of the prose, and the fate of an empire hangs delicately in the balance.

The Ottoman Empire stood at a crossroads, its future written not just in the annals of history, but in the decisions of its leaders. The Loss of Military Edge was not just a predicament—it was a clarion call to either adapt and evolve or to fade into history as a once-mighty giant that could not outpace the shadow of time.

## Administrative Challenges

AT THE HEART OF THE Ottoman Empire's sprawling dominion, an insidious scourge festered, one that would corrode the very foundations upon which the empire stood: bureaucratic inefficiencies and rampant corruption. These twin malaises, pervasive and deep-rooted, were to play a critical role in the empire's slow but inexorable decline throughout the 17th and 18th centuries.

Imagine an empire where the gears of administration grind to a halt, where the hands that should steer the state are instead dipped in the public coffers, pilfering for personal gain. This was the reality for the Ottoman Empire, a realm where the efficient management of extensive territories was paramount for cohesion and strength. Yet, it was this very management that began to fail, an ominous harbinger of a fading titan.

The impact was devastating. With every act of corruption, with every bureaucratic bottleneck, the empire's vitality seeped away. The intricate network of provinces and the complex machinery of imperial governance, once the envy of nations, now stumbled in a quagmire of malfeasance and inertia. The consequences were manifold: tax revenues leaked, public services deteriorated, and the empire's ability to mobilize its resources in times of need was severely undermined.

Consider the tale of an aged tax collector in the province of Anatolia, whose withered hands were known to be as sticky as they were frail. His position, secured through a web of favors and bribes, became a personal fiefdom, where the empire's dues were siphoned to adorn his lavish estate. The villagers, burdened by his greed, lost faith in the empire's justice. Their resentment simmered, a testament to the personal toll such corruption exacted on the empire's citizens.

The stakes could not have been higher. The lifeblood of the empire was being drained, not by the sword of an adversary, but by the pen of the bureaucrat and the greed of the official. As trust in the state eroded, so too did the loyalty of its subjects. The fabric of the empire, woven over centuries, began to unravel.

But within the pages of this book lies more than a lament; it holds the promise of understanding and insight. The reader will be guided through the labyrinth of the Ottoman bureaucracy to grasp the full extent of its failings and to explore the attempts at reform that flickered and died in the shadow of institutional inertia.

The empire's leadership, aware of the rot within, made sporadic attempts to cleanse and streamline the bureaucracy. New regulations were decreed, inspectors were dispatched, and punishments for the corrupt were pronounced. Yet, the implementation of these measures was often stymied by the very corruption they sought to eradicate. The irony was as bitter as it was palpable.

Was it possible for the empire to break free from the stranglehold of its administrative maladies? The answer lay in the hands of those officials who still held fast to a sense of duty and honor. These individuals, though few and far between, represented a flicker of hope, a chance that the tide of decline could be stemmed.

As the narrative unfolds, the reader will be invited to walk the halls of the Sublime Porte, to witness the intrigue and the power plays that shaped the empire's destiny. Through vivid descriptions and a narrative that breathes life into the past, the book will transport one to the very heart of the Ottoman dilemma.

Could the empire have charted a different course? Could the lessons of history serve as a guide for contemporary states facing similar challenges? These are the questions that will engage and provoke, inviting the reader to ponder the intricate dance of power, governance, and human fallibility.

In the chapters to come, the reader will be drawn deeper into the Ottoman world, exploring the reforms attempted by enlightened sultans, the pushback from entrenched interests, and the ultimate fate of an empire unable to reform its administrative body. The journey promises to be one of enlightenment, shedding light on a critical aspect of the empire's history that is often overshadowed by its military exploits and cultural achievements.

The tale of the Ottoman Empire is not just a chronicle of battles and sultans; it is also a story of the silent, creeping decay that can consume a state from within. It is a cautionary tale, a historical study, and, above all, a narrative that resonates with timeless relevance.

## Attempts at Modernization

IN THE WANING YEARS of the 18th century, the Ottoman Empire found itself at a crossroads of survival, grappling with the relentless tide of European advancement. As the West surged forward, buoyed by the winds of the Industrial Revolution, the Ottoman Empire—a once-mighty colossus straddling continents—began to show signs of obsolescence within its institutions, military, and social structures.

Picture the empire's vast territories, teeming with diversity yet bound by age-old traditions, suddenly confronted with the need for profound transformation. It was against this backdrop that the Tanzimat reforms emerged, a series of radical edicts aimed at catapulting the Ottoman state into the modern age.

What were the catalysts that sparked this ambitious undertaking? The empire had suffered humiliating defeats at the hands of technologically superior European armies, its territories eroded by the encroaching powers of Russia, Britain, and France. The society itself, with its myriad ethnicities and religions, clamored for change amidst growing nationalism and the desire for civil liberties. Thus, the Tanzimat period, spanning from 1839 to 1876, marked a pivotal era of feverish reform efforts.

Have you ever wondered how a society entrenched in tradition reacts when the winds of change sweep across its lands? The Tanzimat reforms sought to reshape the empire's legal, military, and educational systems. The Hatt-i Sharif of Gülhane, the noble edict of 1839, set the tone by promising equality among the empire's subjects, regardless of religion or race. It was a bold proclamation that aimed to stem the tide of separatism and foster a sense of Ottoman identity.

Can you imagine the impact of such a declaration? Christians and Jews, long accustomed to secondary status, were granted equal rights under the law. The Millet system, which had allowed for religious autonomy, was reformed to integrate non-Muslim communities more closely into the Ottoman framework. Moreover, the abolition of tax farming and the initiation of a regular taxation system sought to eradicate the deep-seated corruption that had plagued the empire for centuries.

The empire's legal institutions underwent a seismic shift as well. The Mecelle, a codification of Islamic civil law, was introduced to standardize legal proceedings and bring Ottoman jurisprudence in line with European standards. This monumental work spanned over thirty years and consisted of books covering various aspects of civil law, such as property, obligations, and family law.

Turn your gaze to the military, where the modernization efforts were no less dramatic. The Janissary Corps, once the empire's elite soldiers, had become a reactionary force resistant to change. Their dissolution in 1826 paved the way for a new army, trained and equipped along European lines. This reformed military, known as the Asakir-i Mansure-i Muhammediye, was to be a disciplined, professional force, symbolizing the empire's renewed vigor.

But what of the people, the very sinews and muscles of the empire, who bore the brunt of these reforms? The Tanzimat era brought about significant changes in land ownership, with land reforms aimed at creating a loyal, tax-paying peasantry. Education, too, was revolutionized, with the establishment of new schools and the introduction of a state-controlled curriculum designed to produce civil servants loyal to the reformist vision.

However, the path of reform was fraught with challenges. The entrenched elite, whose power was threatened by the changes, resisted vehemently. The ulama, guardians of Islamic law, viewed the reforms with suspicion, fearing the erosion of their influence. Peasants, whose lives were upended by the reorganization of land ownership, often found themselves worse off, fueling discontent.

In the grand tapestry of history, the Tanzimat reforms stand out as a bold attempt to redefine an empire. Yet, the question looms: did these reforms sow the seeds for the empire's eventual dissolution or were they a desperate, ultimately futile, attempt to hold back the tide of history?

As we delve deeper into the annals of the Ottoman Empire, the legacy of the Tanzimat era continues to echo through time. The very fabric of modern Turkey, with its secular legal system and emphasis on nationalism, can trace its roots to this period of transformation. The Tanzimat reforms, for all their imperfections, set the stage for the birth of a new nation-state from the ashes of an empire.

What lessons can be drawn from these attempts at modernization? How does the Ottoman experience inform our understanding of contemporary efforts at reform in the face of entrenched traditionalism and resistance to change?

The story of the Ottoman Empire's attempts at modernization is one of ambition, struggle, and paradox. It is a narrative that offers a window into the heart of a civilization in flux, a civilization striving to redefine itself amidst the inexorable march of time. Let us continue to unspool the threads of this rich historical tapestry, revealing the shades and nuances of an empire's quest for renewal.

## Economic Difficulties

THROUGHOUT THE OTTOMAN Empire, the shimmering mirage of wealth and prosperity often obscured the underlying fragility of its economic foundations. It is here, nestled within the complex weave of history, that we uncover the financial adversities that beset this once-majestic realm.

Imagine a world where the opulence of sultans belied the creeping shadow of debt. The Ottoman economy, much like the intricate patterns of a Persian rug, revealed upon closer inspection the frayed threads of fiscal distress. The empire's coffers, once brimming with the spoils of conquest, began to hemorrhage under the relentless pressures of modern economic warfare.

What was the crux of this economic malaise? At its heart lay an empire struggling to navigate the uncharted waters of a global economy, where the mercantile prowess of European powers cast a long and ominous shadow over traditional trade routes. The Ottoman Empire, which had once thrived on the lucrative trade between East and West, found itself grappling with trade imbalances that threatened to capsize its economy.

The evidence of these struggles is etched within the voluminous ledgers of European financiers. By the 19th century, the empire had become increasingly dependent on foreign loans, with each successive borrowing deepening the quagmire of debt. Like a gambler ensnared by the illusion of a winning streak, the Ottoman state borrowed heavily to fund ambitious modernization projects, military campaigns, and the luxurious lifestyle of its elite.

Let us delve deeper into the financial morass that ensnared the empire. The Capitulations, agreements with European powers granting them significant economic privileges, compounded the fiscal woes. These concessions eroded the empire's sovereignty over its own trade, allowing European merchants to dominate commerce, often at the expense of local producers. This influx of foreign goods stifled domestic industries, leaving the empire's economy vulnerable to external shocks.

Yet, a counter-narrative suggests that the Capitulations were not solely to blame. Some historians argue that these agreements facilitated the flow of foreign capital and technology into the empire, fostering economic growth in certain sectors. Could the empire have leveraged these opportunities to its advantage?

However, the counter-evidence pales against the stark reality of the empire's financial decline. The reliance on foreign loans created a vicious cycle of debt, where new loans were procured to service existing debts, further eroding the empire's fiscal autonomy. The Public Debt Administration, established by European creditors to collect the empire's indebted revenues, became a symbol of its economic subjugation.

But there was more to the empire's economic difficulties than debt alone. Tax collection methods remained archaic, and corruption was rife among tax collectors, siphoning off much-needed revenue. Attempts at reform, such as the introduction of a uniform tax system, encountered resistance from entrenched interests and failed to stem the tide of fiscal decline.

In support of the claim that the empire's economy was on a precipice, one needs only to look at the balance of trade. The Ottoman market was flooded with European goods, while traditional exports like silk and spices faced declining demand. The result was a chronic trade deficit that drained the empire's reserves of precious metals, further undermining its monetary stability.

As we weave together these strands of evidence, the picture of an empire caught in an economic maelstrom becomes clearer. The financial struggles of the Ottoman Empire were not merely a symptom of internal mismanagement but were exacerbated by the forces of global capitalism and imperial competition.

In conclusion, it is evident that the Ottoman Empire's economic difficulties were a mosaic of complex and interrelated issues. The burden of debt, trade imbalances, and the Capitulations formed a triad of challenges that sapped the empire's vitality. These economic adversities cast long shadows over the empire's political and social landscape, contributing to its eventual unraveling.

As historians, we must scrutinize the past with diligence, for it is within the crumbling ledgers of empires that we glean lessons for the future. The economic trials of the Ottoman Empire serve as a cautionary tale of the perils of fiscal imprudence and the harsh realities of a world economy. As we continue to unfurl the sagas of empires, let us ponder the enduring relevance of these economic parables, for they hold the keys to understanding the intricate dance between power and prosperity.

# Rise of Nationalism

WITHIN THE LABYRINTHINE history of the Ottoman Empire, a new force began to stir, one that would eventually unravel the intricate tapestry of imperial rule. This force was nationalism, a term that evokes powerful emotions and complex ideologies. At its core, nationalism is the belief that a people who share common cultural, linguistic, or ethnic characteristics should have the right to form a sovereign nation-state.

Nationalism germinated in the fertile soil of the Enlightenment and the French Revolution, where the seeds of self-determination and democracy were sown. As these ideas took root, they began to challenge the age-old hierarchies and loyalties that had long governed empires and kingdoms. In the Ottoman context, nationalism became both a rallying cry and a death knell, as different ethnic groups sought their place in the sun, free from the yoke of imperial dominion.

The key elements of nationalism include a shared sense of identity, a collective memory or myth of common ancestry, and the desire for political autonomy or independence. Often, these elements are galvanized by charismatic leaders, historical events, or cultural renaissance, leading to the creation of nationalist movements. In the Ottoman Empire, these movements arose among various ethnic groups, including Greeks, Serbs, Bulgarians, and Armenians, each with their own unique aspirations and grievances.

Historically, the concept of nationalism is relatively modern, gaining prominence in the 19th century as empires faced the dual threats of internal dissent and external competition. In the case of the Ottoman Empire, nationalism's rise can be traced back to the impact of the Napoleonic Wars and the spread of revolutionary ideas. The empire's diverse population, once held together by the common bond of Islam and the sultan's authority, began to fracture along ethnic lines.

Contextualizing within a broader framework, the Ottoman Empire was not alone in facing the challenges posed by nationalism. Across Europe, empires and dynasties confronted similar struggles, as subjects sought to redefine the basis of political legitimacy and governance. The Habsburgs, Romanovs, and Hohenzollerns all grappled with the upsurge of nationalist sentiment within their realms.

Real-world applications of these nationalist movements were evident in the numerous revolts and uprisings that punctuated the 19th century. The Greek War of Independence (1821-1830) serves as a prime example, where the desire for self-rule led to the establishment of a sovereign Greek state. The subsequent waves of nationalism led to the gradual disintegration of the Ottoman territories in Europe, as more and more regions broke away to form independent nations.

However, common misconceptions about nationalism within the Ottoman Empire suggest that it was a homogeneous force with uniform effects. On the contrary, nationalism manifested in diverse ways, influenced by local conditions, historical experiences, and international dynamics. Some nationalist movements sought outright independence, while others initially pursued autonomy within the empire.

The narratives of nationalism are painted in vivid hues of courage, betrayal, hope, and despair. Picture the clandestine meetings of intellectuals in smoky coffee houses, the fervent declarations of rebels emboldened by the promise of freedom, and the oppressive response of an empire struggling to maintain its authority. These scenes encapsulate the tumultuous relationship between nationalism and imperial rule.

Do you see the irony in the empire's response to these nationalist movements? The attempts to suppress them often only fueled the flames of resistance, proving the adage that oppression begets rebellion. Ottoman reforms such as the Tanzimat, which aimed to modernize and centralize the empire's administration, inadvertently reinforced nationalist sentiments by promoting a sense of unity and identity among disparate groups.

Yet, one must not overlook the complexities and contradictions inherent in nationalist ideologies. Nationalism, while advocating for the rights of a particular group, frequently marginalized or oppressed other communities within the same territory. The dark shadow of ethnic cleansing and inter-communal violence often accompanied the noble aspirations of nationhood, a stark reminder of the duality of human endeavors.

In a concise reflection on the rise of nationalism within the Ottoman Empire, it becomes clear that the forces unleashed by this potent ideology were instrumental in reshaping the political map of the region. The demise of the empire was not merely the result of external conquests but also the internal corrosion wrought by the quest for national identity and self-determination.

As we continue to navigate the intricate corridors of history, let us pause to consider the enduring legacy of nationalism. Its impact is still felt today, as nations grapple with the balancing act between unity and diversity, between the desire for self-rule and the demands of a globalized world. Through the lens of the Ottoman experience, we gain insight into the transformative power of nationalism—a force capable of forging nations from the empires' ashes.

# Decline and Dissolution

## The Young Turk Revolution

In the waning days of the 19th century, the once-mighty Ottoman Empire was a shadow of its former self, a sprawling, anachronistic colossus straining under the weight of internal strife and external pressures. It was a time of simmering discontent, of fervent nationalism within its diverse territories, and of predatory interests by foreign powers eager to carve out a piece of the declining empire.

The dawn of the 20th century witnessed the stirrings of change—change that came to be known as the Young Turk Revolution. A movement cloaked in secrecy and driven by a cadre of determined military officers and intellectuals, it arose from the embers of frustration with Sultan Abdul Hamid II's autocratic rule. These Young Turks, as they were soon called, yearned for the resurrection of the constitution which promised equality and justice, and they were prepared to challenge the very foundations of the empire to see their aspirations realized.

It was July 1908 when the revolution erupted. As if carried on the midsummer winds, the fervor spread swiftly through the ranks of the Third Army in Macedonia. The demands were clear: the restoration of the 1876 constitution and the convening of a parliament. Sultan Abdul Hamid II, sensing the shifting tides and the potential for his own demise, capitulated. The constitution was reinstated, and the empire was ostensibly transformed overnight from an absolute monarchy to a constitutional one. But the question lingered in the smoke-filled coffee houses and within the grand halls of power alike: would this revolution truly herald the dawn of a new era?

Consider for a moment the profound sense of hope that must have filled the hearts of many. The promises of the Young Turks were not just political; they were a beacon of modernization, a path to a revitalized empire that might once again command respect on the world stage. They envisioned an Ottoman society that would embrace science, education, and industry, one that would shrug off the 'sick man of Europe' moniker and stride confidently into the 20th century.

Yet, as we cast our gaze through the lens of history, we must ask ourselves: how did these lofty ideals fare in the crucible of reality? How did such a promising revolution lead to an empire embroiled in the Great War just a few years later? And what lessons can we glean from the Young Turk Revolution that resonate in our own times, as we grapple with the complexities of governance, identity, and modernity?

History, when carefully examined, reveals its intricate web connecting past to present. The Young Turk Revolution, with its blend of hope and upheaval, offers a poignant example. The issues it sought to address—nationalism, democracy, social reform—continue to challenge the modern nation-states that emerged from the Ottoman Empire's ashes. The revolution's aftermath, marked by both achievements and tragedies, serves as a sobering reminder of the often unpredictable nature of sweeping political change.

And so, dear reader, as we delve into the heart of this story, let us consider the enduring significance of the Young Turk Revolution. It is a tale not merely of a political upheaval but also of human ambition and frailty, of the quest for progress and the specter of hubris. It is a chapter in the annals of history that stands as a testament to the complexity of the human condition—a chapter that we must understand if we are to navigate the tumultuous waters of our own era with wisdom and foresight.

The empire's struggle and the revolution's fiery spirit echo through time, whispering to us that the past is not a distant shore, but the soil beneath our feet, fertile with lessons for today and seeds for tomorrow's harvest. Let us then embark on this journey together, exploring the intricate dance of history as it unfolds across the stage of the Ottoman Empire, and perhaps, in its reflection, we may glean insights into our own world's unfolding drama.

## Balkan Wars and Territorial Losses

AS THE NEW CENTURY dawned, the Ottoman Empire's grip on its territories weakened, and the winds of change carried the scent of impending conflict. The Balkan region, a mosaic of ethnicities and interests, became the crucible of a crisis that would test the resolve of the Young Turks' reformed empire. The Balkan Wars, a sequence of two conflicts that ravaged the region in 1912 and 1913, laid bare the empire's vulnerabilities and marked a significant turning point in its history.

Before diving into the tumultuous events of the Balkan Wars, let us acquaint ourselves with the main actors on this stage. The Ottoman Empire, despite its recent constitutional reforms, was an aging power struggling to maintain its authority over a diverse realm. Opposing it were the Balkan League, an alliance of burgeoning nation-states—Serbia, Greece, Bulgaria, and Montenegro—each driven by nationalistic fervor and a thirst for territorial expansion at the expense of the weakening empire.

The core challenge for the Ottoman Empire was immense: to preserve its sovereignty over the Balkan territories amid escalating tensions and the aggressive ambitions of its neighbors. Nationalistic uprisings had already been a recurring headache for the empire, but the Balkan Wars represented an existential threat—a coordinated assault by multiple adversaries determined to redraw the map of Europe.

The Ottoman strategy was reactionary and fragmented, hampered by internal political divisions and a lack of resources. The empire's military tactics, once feared across continents, were now outdated and outmatched by the more dynamic and determined armies of the Balkan League. The empire's leadership failed to anticipate the intensity of the onslaught or the unity of its adversaries, leading to a series of catastrophic defeats.

The results were devastating. After the First Balkan War, the Ottoman Empire lost almost all of its European territories, and the Treaty of London (1913) formalized these losses. The Second Balkan War, ignited by disputes among the victors of the first, culminated in the Treaty of Bucharest, which further delineated new borders, significantly reducing Bulgaria's gains but leaving the Ottoman Empire with even less. The empire's territory in Europe shrank to a small area around the city of Istanbul, and its influence in the Balkans all but evaporated.

In reflecting on these events, it is impossible not to consider the broader implications. The empire's territorial losses were not just a blow to its landholdings; they symbolized the fracturing of an imperial identity that had lasted for centuries. The losses also foreshadowed the empire's ultimate fragmentation, which would be hastened by the even greater cataclysm of the First World War.

While visual aids such as maps of pre-and post-war territorial boundaries would further elucidate the scale of the empire's losses, let us not forget the human cost. The wars displaced hundreds of thousands, leaving deep scars on the collective memory of the region's peoples—scars that, in some cases, have yet to heal.

The story of the Balkan Wars is inseparable from the larger narrative of the Ottoman Empire's decline. These wars serve as a stark reminder that empires, regardless of their might and longevity, are not immune to the forces of nationalism and the desire for self-determination.

As we close this chapter on the Balkan Wars and their aftermath, one must ponder the nature of empires and the lessons their rises and falls impart. How often does the quest for power and expansion sow the seeds of an empire's undoing? And what can the modern world, with its complex web of nation-states, learn from the ashes of empires past?

The Ottoman Empire's experience in the Balkans invites us to reflect on these questions. It urges us to consider the enduring cycle of conflict and transformation that shapes our history and the world we know today. As we turn the page, let us carry with us the understanding that the past is not merely a record of events but a mirror reflecting our own struggles and aspirations. What, then, might the reflection of the Balkan Wars reveal about our current age, and how might we use these reflections to shape a more peaceful future?

# World War I and the Ottomans

IN THE WAKE OF THE Balkan Wars, the Ottoman Empire, the once formidable dominion of sultans, stood diminished and vulnerable. Its European territories were a shadow of their former glory, and the empire's future seemed to hang in the balance. Yet, it was within this crucible of defeat and despair that World War I would offer the Ottomans an unexpected opportunity to reclaim some measure of power and prestige.

The genesis of the Ottoman Empire's involvement in the Great War was intricately tied to its quest for survival. As the war clouds gathered over Europe in 1914, the empire sought to align itself with the powers that could offer the most favorable terms for its own territorial integrity and sovereignty. This pragmatic approach led the Ottomans to form an alliance with the Central Powers, consisting of Germany and Austria-Hungary, setting the stage for a campaign that would etch itself into the annals of military history.

The Gallipoli Campaign, also known as the Battle of Çanakkale, emerged as one of the most significant milestones for the Ottomans during the war. Intended as a bold move by the Allied Forces to secure a sea route to Russia, the campaign quickly spiraled into a protracted and grueling conflict, with the Ottoman forces displaying an unexpected and tenacious resistance. The shores of Gallipoli became a hallowed battleground, soaked in the blood of countless soldiers, as the Ottomans fought tooth and nail against the invaders.

Under the leadership of Mustafa Kemal, who would later be known as Atatürk, the father of modern Turkey, the Ottoman troops held their ground. The Allies' dreams of a swift victory were swallowed by the rugged terrain and the fierce spirit of Ottoman defiance. Gallipoli became a symbol of national pride, a testament to the empire's resilience in the face of seemingly insurmountable odds.

Envision the trenches carved into the earth, the deafening roar of artillery, and the solemn faces of soldiers resigned to a fate shrouded in gunpowder and uncertainty. The Gallipoli Campaign was not merely a clash of armies; it was a crucible where the identity of a nation was forged from the flames of conflict.

And what of the broader war? Across distant lands and seas, the Ottoman Empire's forces engaged in battles that would shape the borders and destinies of nations. In the deserts of the Middle East, the empire faced the Arab Revolt and the machinations of British officer T.E. Lawrence, known as Lawrence of Arabia. The empire's territories became arenas for modern warfare, with the specter of colonial ambition and the thirst for oil looming over the theater of combat.

The cultural and regional variations in the empire's approach to war were stark. In the Arab provinces, the Ottoman authorities grappled with internal dissent and the complex web of tribal alliances. In the Caucasus, they faced the Russians in harsh, unforgiving landscapes. Each front brought unique challenges, testing the mettle of Ottoman leadership and strategy.

As the war dragged on, the strains on the empire grew ever more acute. Resources dwindled, and the populace groaned under the weight of sacrifice and loss. The once mighty Ottoman war machine was pushed to its limits, and cracks began to appear in the empire's façade of unity.

The modern interpretations of the Ottoman Empire's role in World War I are diverse and often contentious. Some view the empire's participation as a noble stand against imperial aggression, while others see it as a final, desperate grasp at power by a decaying dynasty. The controversies surrounding events like the Armenian Genocide add layers of complexity to our understanding of the period, forcing us to confront the darkest chapters of history with honesty and a commitment to seeking truth.

As the war concluded with the signing of the Armistice of Mudros in 1918, the Ottoman Empire faced the inevitable: defeat and dissolution. The Treaty of Sèvres, though later supplanted by the Treaty of Lausanne, carved up the empire's remaining territories, giving birth to the modern states of the Middle East and setting the stage for a century of turmoil and transformation.

As we reflect on the echoes of the Ottoman war drums, faded now into the silence of history, we must ask ourselves: How did the empire's fall reshape the world we know? What lessons can we glean from the rubble of empires, and how do we apply these lessons to the conflicts that continue to plague our modern age?

The story of the Ottoman Empire in World War I is a tapestry of valor and tragedy, of ambition and folly. It is a narrative that invites us to ponder the ebb and flow of human fortunes and the enduring quest for national identity and sovereignty. As the last whispers of the empire faded into the annals of time, a new chapter was written, one that continues to influence the geopolitical landscape to this very day. Let us remember the Ottomans not just for their final battles, but for the rich tapestry of history they wove, a legacy that endures in the spirit of the nations that rose from their ashes.

# The Armenian Genocide

IN THE SHADOW OF THE Gallipoli Campaign and the wider Great War, a tragedy unfolded that would forever mar the legacy of the Ottoman Empire. Even as the empire's soldiers fought valiantly on distant fronts, within its own borders, the architects of despair were drafting a blueprint for annihilation. This was the Armenian Genocide, a cataclysm that would claim the lives of an estimated 1.5 million Armenians and spawn a legacy of sorrow and strife that lingers to this day.

Imagine a land where the echo of ancient civilizations still whispered through the valleys and mountains—a place where diverse cultures had coexisted for centuries under the dominion of empires. Armenians, an indigenous people of the Anatolian plateau, had called this land home long before the rise of the Ottomans. With the fall of Constantinople in 1453 and the expansion of Ottoman control, Armenians found themselves subjects of a new empire, one that would oscillate between tolerance and repression over the centuries.

As the 20th century dawned, the Ottoman Empire was a mix of ethnicities and religions, with Armenians predominantly inhabiting the eastern provinces. However, the winds of change—nationalism, modernization, and the empire's decline—were fanning the flames of ethnic tension. The Young Turk Revolution of 1908 promised reform and equality, but it also brought to power a faction that harbored a darker vision for the empire's future—a vision that did not include the Armenians.

Why did this vision take such a sinister turn? The answer lies partly in the empire's crumbling facade. The loss in the Balkan Wars and the fear of further territorial disintegration bred a toxic nationalism that sought to homogenize the empire's population. The Armenians, perceived as a fifth column due to their Christian faith and alleged sympathies with Russian adversaries, became scapegoats for the empire's ills.

As World War I raged, the Ottoman government, now under the sway of the Committee of Union and Progress (CUP), seized the moment to address what they called the "Armenian Question." On April 24, 1915, hundreds of Armenian intellectuals and leaders were arrested in Constantinople, marking the beginning of a meticulously organized campaign of extermination.

The brutality that ensued was unspeakable. Men, women, and children were uprooted from their homes, forced into death marches across the Syrian Desert, deprived of food and water, and subjected to robbery, rape, and massacre. The once-vibrant Armenian communities were systematically dismantled, their cultural heritage laid to waste. Can you fathom the deafening silence where once there was the hum of life?

This history, as dark and unfathomable as it may be, casts a long shadow over our present world. The repercussions of the Armenian Genocide are manifold, influencing contemporary geopolitics, international law, and human rights discourse. The persistent denial of the genocide by successive Turkish governments has added a complex layer to international relations, particularly with Armenia and the Armenian diaspora.

Why does this history matter now? Because the refusal to acknowledge past atrocities impedes reconciliation and healing. It hinders our collective ability to prevent future massacres and genocides. Understanding the Armenian Genocide is not just an academic exercise; it is a moral imperative that challenges us to stand against the currents of denial and revisionism.

But let us not forget the resilience of the human spirit. Despite the attempts to erase them from history, the Armenian people have persevered. Their diaspora communities around the world are a testament to their enduring culture and resolve. The genocide, while a defining tragedy, is not the end of their story but a chapter in a narrative of survival and renewal.

The journey from the historical depths of the Armenian Genocide to the ongoing quest for recognition and justice is fraught with obstacles. It is a journey that requires us to confront uncomfortable truths, to empathize with the pain of others, and to learn from the past so that we may forge a more just and compassionate future.

This book, 'The Ottoman Empire,' is more than a recounting of lost empires and bygone battles. It is an invitation to understand the complexity of human history, to recognize the threads of continuity that bind our past to our present, and to realize that the struggles of yesterday are inextricably linked to the challenges we face today.

## The Birth of the Republic of Turkey

AFTER THE OTTOMAN DEFEAT in World War I, the Empire was carved up by the victorious Allied powers, but Mustafa Kemal galvanized the remnants of the Ottoman army and the Turkish people to resist foreign occupation and dismemberment.

Picture the remnants of a once-glorious empire, now a nation in shackles, its people longing for salvation. Atatürk, a visionary and a military genius, emerged from the ashes of war to ignite the flame of independence. Through a series of military campaigns and diplomatic maneuvers, he successfully expelled foreign forces and nullified the humiliating terms of the Treaty of Sèvres.

In the wake of victory, the question loomed: What would replace the fallen empire? The answer was revolutionary. The Sultanate was abolished in 1922, and the Caliphate followed in 1924, severing the millennia-old tie between political authority and religious leadership. The proclamation of the Republic in 1923 was not merely a change of government; it was a profound cultural and societal revolution.

Atatürk's vision for Turkey was radical. He aspired to create a modern, progressive state, anchored in the West rather than the East. Can you imagine the audacity of replacing the Arabic script with the Latin alphabet, or the courage required to grant women the right to vote and stand for office in a society deeply rooted in tradition?

Atatürk's reforms touched every aspect of life: the legal system, education, language, attire, and even the calendar. He introduced the Gregorian calendar, Sunday as the day of rest, and the metric system. Secularism was aggressively promoted; the fez, a symbol of Ottoman identity, was banned; and religious attire was discouraged in public offices.

The essence of Atatürk's Principles was to forge a new Turkish identity. Nationalism was redefined to create a sense of unity and purpose, while statism emphasized the role of the state in economic development. These principles, enshrined in the very fabric of the Republic, were meant to propel Turkey into the modern age.

Do these reforms imply that the transition was smooth or universally accepted? Far from it. Atatürk faced opposition from traditionalists, religious leaders, and ethnic minorities. Yet, through a combination of political acumen and authoritarian control, he managed to implement his vision.

Let us bear in mind the significance of Atatürk's legacy. His efforts to create a secular, Western-oriented Republic from the remnants of the Ottoman Empire set the stage for the complex and often tumultuous evolution of modern Turkey. While the Republic has evolved in the decades since Atatürk's death, the imprint of his reforms continues to shape Turkish society and politics.

# Legacy of the Empire

## Cultural Heritage

Throughout history, few empires have managed to weave as rich and enduring a cultural heritage as the Ottoman Empire. Its threads have stretched across centuries, leaving an indelible mark on the fabric of numerous societies. From the bustling bazaars of Istanbul to the cuisine that has tantalized palates worldwide, the empire's legacy is a testament to its once vast dominion.

The grandeur of Ottoman art and architecture is not merely a subject of admiration but a narrative of cultural synthesis. But what is it about these artistic expressions that continue to captivate? It is the meticulous attention to detail, the dedication to craftsmanship, and the boldness in design that underpins the empire's aesthetic contributions. Each archway and arabesque tells a story of cultural exchange, of artisans who embraced diverse influences and molded them into something uniquely Ottoman.

How has this heritage persevered in the lands that once fell under the empire's sway? One need only wander through the old quarters of Sarajevo or the stone-paved alleys of Jerusalem to witness the living museums of Ottoman architecture. The caravanserais still stand, echoing the footsteps of ancient travelers, while the public baths continue to offer solace, as they have for centuries.

Delving deeper, one discovers the subtle flavors of Ottoman cuisine still relished in the region's culinary traditions. The spicy zest of Turkish kebabs, the honeyed layers of baklava, and the robust aroma of Greek coffee—each a remnant of a culinary heritage that knew no boundaries. These dishes are not mere sustenance but an abundance of tastes that mirror the empire's multicultural ethos.

Is it not remarkable how the empire's culinary repertoire, much like its art, was a crucible of various regional influences? The Ottoman kitchen was a place of innovation, where chefs from the Balkans to the Middle East contributed their local ingredients and techniques to create a fusion that is celebrated to this day.

Yet, beyond aesthetics and appetites, the Ottoman legacy is also etched in the legal and social frameworks of its former territories. It introduced administrative systems and legal reforms that have outlasted the empire itself. Can we then measure the impact of such heritage solely through visible monuments and tangible artifacts? Or does it extend into the intangible ethos of societies shaped by centuries of Ottoman rule?

The empire's cultural footprint is also quantifiable. Scholars have labored to chart the influence of Ottoman art, meticulously documenting the spread of motifs and styles across different mediums and regions. They have traced the lineage of recipes that have crossed continents, adapting to local palates while retaining their Ottoman soul.

In understanding such a complex heritage, one must navigate the intricacies of history with care. For instance, the term "Ottoman" itself encapsulates a multitude of ethnicities, languages, and traditions. How, then, does one distill the essence of an empire whose very nature was diverse and dynamic?

The answer lies not in simplification but in the celebration of this diversity. For it is in the variety of its cultural expressions that the true spirit of the Ottoman legacy is revealed. We see it in Millet systems attempt to bring about the coexistence of mosque, church, and synagogue; in the dialogues of poets and scholars who found refuge within its borders; and in the enduring symbols of an empire that once bridged East and West.

As we arrive at the conclusion of this exploration, we are reminded that the Ottoman Empire's cultural heritage is not a relic of the past but a living, breathing influence on the present. It is a legacy that continues to inspire artists, tantalize chefs, and shape societies. It is a reminder that empires may crumble, but their cultural contributions can endure, transcending the annals of history to touch the lives of generations to come.

Thus, we are left to ponder: How will we carry forward the richness of Ottoman heritage? How will we weave these threads into our own cultural narratives? And, most importantly, how will we ensure that the legacy of this once-mighty empire remains not just in the echoes of its past glory but in the vibrant, evolving story of our shared human history?

# Modern Turkey

IN THE SHADOWS OF A bygone empire, Modern Turkey stands, a nation eternally linked to its illustrious Ottoman past yet ceaselessly marching towards a future carved by the secular reforms of Mustafa Kemal Atatürk. This transformation from a sultan's realm to a democratic republic is not merely a political shift but a cultural metamorphosis that has redefined a society.

The Republic of Turkey and the Ottoman Empire embody concepts of governance and culture that, while rooted in the same soil, have blossomed into distinct entities. The significance of such a comparison is not lost on those who seek to understand the intricate dance of tradition and modernity.

In this analysis, the benchmarks for comparison are set by the pivotal realms of political structure, cultural identity, and societal norms. By these standards, we can discern how the shadow of the

Ottoman crescent moon still casts its presence over the star of the Turkish republic.

The similarities between the two are woven through the fabric of Turkish society. The Ottoman influence is palpable in the nation's legal codes, language, and even in the collective memory of its people, who still revere the empire's former greatness. Both the empire and the republic have shown a propensity for strong, centralized leadership, as seen in the sultans of old and the revered figure of Atatürk.

Yet, the distinctions are equally profound. The Ottoman Empire was a theocracy, with the sultan holding both political and religious authority, whereas the Republic of Turkey was founded on the principles of secularism and nationalism, deliberately separating religion from state affairs.

The visual contrast between Istanbul's minarets reaching for the sky and Ankara's bureaucratic edifices rooted in practical governance is symbolic of the wider dichotomy between the two eras. One was an empire looking to conquer; the other, a republic aspiring to join the league of modern nations.

The reforms of Atatürk, which included the adoption of a new legal system, the Latin alphabet, and the prohibition of fez and veil, highlight a deliberate move away from past Ottoman customs. These actions were not simply legislative changes but a rebranding of a nation's identity, a cultural revolution that sought to sweep away the vestiges of imperial rule.

But what do these comparisons reveal? They speak of a nation's struggle with its own soul, caught between the allure of its imperial majesty and the pragmatic needs of a modern state. Turkey's current political landscape, with its oscillation between authoritarianism and democracy, reflects the enduring tension between these identities.

How does this historical analysis relate to the present? The echoes of the Ottoman past are heard in the current political discourse of Turkey, with some invoking the empire's legacy to bolster a sense of nationalism, while others warn against the dangers of romanticizing a past incompatible with contemporary democratic values.

As the nation ponders its future, questions arise. Can the Republic of Turkey uphold Atatürk's vision of a secular state while acknowledging its Ottoman heritage? How does this duality shape Turkey's role on the global stage?

With each passing day, the pages of history turn, revealing new chapters in the story of a nation perpetually balancing the weight of its imperial history with the ambitions of its republican present. The legacy of the Ottoman Empire, with its grandeur and complexity, remains not just in the grand mosques and palaces but in the nuanced fabric of Turkish society.

Thus, as the sun sets on the domes of Istanbul, casting long shadows over the Bosphorus, one is left to wonder: will the star of modern Turkey shine bright enough to illuminate its path forward, or will the shadows of its Ottoman past lengthen, shaping its journey in ways yet to be seen?

Modern Turkey, a land of contrasts, a bridge between continents and epochs, continues to define itself through a dance with its history. The story of this nation is a living testament to the enduring influence of an empire long gone and a republic's steadfast march towards its own destiny.

## Influence on the Balkans

WHISPERS OF A BYGONE era linger in the cobbled streets and ancient fortresses of the Balkans. Here, amidst verdant hills and sapphire seas, the legacy of the Ottoman Empire endures, woven into the very fabric of society. To understand the complexities of this influence is to journey through a path of cultural syncretism, political upheaval, and social transformation.

The main players in this historical drama are the diverse peoples of the Balkans—Bosniaks, Serbs, Croats, Albanians, and Greeks—who, despite their distinct identities, share a common thread in their histories: the centuries-long presence of the Ottoman Empire. Their ancestors were subjects of sultans, soldiers in imperial armies, and artisans in bazaars that teemed with a blend of Byzantine, Slavic, and Oriental motifs.

The challenge at the heart of this narrative is the enduring Ottoman influence amidst the region's quest for national identity and sovereignty. Where once the Sultan's word was law, new nations have emerged, each forging its path while grappling with the shadows of empire.

The Ottoman administrative and landholding systems, once the backbone of imperial control, left an indelible mark on Balkan societies. Strategies for dealing with this legacy varied from country to country: some sought to dismantle the feudal structures, while others adapted them to fit new national frameworks. The results of these approaches have shaped the region's socio-political landscape, from agrarian reform to urban planning.

Perhaps the most striking outcome of Ottoman influence is the religious and cultural diversity of the Balkans. Islam, introduced by the Ottomans, remains a major faith in the region, interwoven with Christian denominations. This religious tapestry, though rich, has also been a source of tension, as seen in the tragic conflicts of the late 20th century. Yet, it is also a testament to a shared history that continues to shape communal relations.

Reflecting on this case study, one must acknowledge the criticisms of those who view the Ottoman legacy through the lens of oppression and decline. Yet, it is also important to recognize the contributions to architecture, cuisine, music, and language that have enriched Balkan cultures.

Visual aids, such as the intricate tile work of a mosque or the preserved cobblestone bazaar, serve as tangible reminders of the empire's aesthetic contributions. Maps delineating the shifting borders illustrate the geopolitical transformations spurred by the Ottoman retreat and the subsequent Balkan Wars.

Connecting these details to the larger narrative, it is clear that the Ottoman past is not a mere footnote but an enduring chapter in the story of the Balkans. The region's current political dynamics, cultural diversity, and social issues are inextricably linked to its Ottoman inheritance.

As we turn the page on this exploration, one might ponder: How will the Balkans continue to reconcile its multicultural legacy with the push for national homogeneity? Will the shared Ottoman history serve as a bridge for cooperation or a battleground for division?

The echoes of the Ottoman Empire in the Balkans are a reminder that history's influence is not confined to textbooks but lives on in the daily lives of people. As the sun sets over the Adriatic, casting a golden glow on the remnants of fortresses and mosques, the Balkans stand as a living museum, a chronicle of an empire's lasting impact on a region at the crossroads of history.

# Middle Eastern Borders

THE DUST HAS LONG SETTLED on the once-mighty Ottoman Empire, yet its legacy casts a long shadow over the modern Middle East. The empire's dissolution, a seismic event in early 20th-century history, catalyzed the drawing of new national borders. A mixture of peoples, cultures, and religions, once unified under the Ottoman banner, found themselves divided by lines on a map, often drawn by foreign hands indifferent to the intricate tapestry of local identities. It is within this framework that we explore the genesis of contemporary conflicts and the quest for solutions to the region's most intractable challenges.

At the heart of the present turmoil lies a profound predicament: the borders carved out of the Empire's remains have trapped diverse groups within nation-states ill-suited to their historical and sociopolitical realities. Arbitrary borders, drawn without heed to the centuries-old bonds of community and the schisms of sect, have sown the seeds of discord. The Sykes-Picot Agreement of 1916 stands as a testament to this legacy—a secret pact that shaped destinies with the stroke of a pen.

The repercussions of this geopolitical division resonate to this day. Nations have been plunged into turmoil, with internal factions vying for power, autonomy, or outright independence. From the Kurdish struggle that spreads across multiple countries to the sectarian strife in Iraq, the artificiality of these borders has fueled a seemingly endless cycle of conflict. The specter of such discord looms large, threatening not just the stability of the Middle East but that of the entire world, as the tentacles of these conflicts reach far beyond their epicenters.

Yet, amidst the turmoil, hope persists. The solution to these deep-seated issues may lie in a reimagining of sovereignty and governance. Decentralization and federalism present themselves as viable pathways to appease the clashing national and cultural identities constrained within the existing state structures. By granting greater autonomy to distinct groups, these systems could alleviate the pressures that threaten to tear nations apart from within.

Implementing such strategies requires a delicate balance between national integrity and local autonomy. One must consider the example of the United Arab Emirates—a federation that has successfully managed to unite disparate emirates while allowing for a degree of local governance. Learning from this model, Middle Eastern states could develop a framework for a more inclusive and flexible system of self-governance, tailored to the unique fabric of each country.

Evidence of the efficacy of this approach can be found by casting an eye towards the past. The millet system of the Ottoman Empire, though not without its flaws, allowed for a certain level of self-administration among different religious and ethnic groups. In a modern context, this could translate into a system where diverse communities have a say in their affairs while still contributing to the broader national narrative.

Are there alternatives to federalism and decentralization? Some advocate for entirely redrawing the map, creating new nations along ethno-sectarian lines. Yet, this carries the risk of perpetuating the cycle of conflict, as it is nearly impossible to draw borders that satisfy all parties. Others propose the strengthening of supranational entities like the Arab League to foster cooperation and collective security. However, this too is fraught with challenges, given the divergent interests of its member states.

As we traverse this landscape of uncertainty and potential, it is crucial to remember that the solutions we seek must be grounded in the realities of the Middle East's diverse societies. They must arise from the people themselves, through dialogue and consensus, rather than imposed from outside. The international community's role should be that of a facilitator, providing support and mediation where necessary but always with respect for the region's sovereign right to self-determination.

The Middle Eastern borders, as they stand, are a patchwork of historical circumstance and political expediency, a legacy of empires and agreements that have long since lost their relevance. Yet, within this patchwork lies the possibility of a new tapestry, woven from the threads of compromise, understanding, and shared destiny.

What remains to be seen is whether the leaders and peoples of the Middle East can rise to this challenge. Can they craft a new narrative, one in which borders are bridges rather than barriers? The journey is fraught with obstacles, but the rewards—a Middle East at peace with itself and its neighbors—are too great to ignore.

History whispers to us from the sands and cities that once thrived under Ottoman rule, urging us to learn from the past as we build the future. The Middle East stands at a crossroads once more, and the paths it chooses will resonate through the ages. Will it be said that in the wake of the Ottoman Empire, new nations emerged, not from the ashes of conflict but from the fertile ground of cooperation and unity? Only time will tell, but the pen that writes the next chapter is in the hands of those who dare to imagine a different world.

## Ottoman Legacy in Law and Governance

IN THE INTRICATE DANCE of history, the Ottoman Empire's choreography of law and governance continues to echo in the halls of modernity. The Empire, a crucible of legal and administrative innovation, left indelible marks on the region's contemporary governance. It is within this historical context that we delve into the unyielding influence of Ottoman legal traditions and their enduring relevance to the political tapestry of today's Middle East.

At the core of this exploration lies the profound assertion that the Ottoman Empire's legal and administrative systems not only shaped the socio-political landscapes of its time but also laid a foundation that continues to undergird legal frameworks in the region. The Millet system, an Ottoman invention, attempted to provide religious communities with a degree of autonomy, allowing them to govern their own civil matters. This historical precedent offers a compelling lens through which modern governance can be viewed and understood.

The primary evidence supporting this claim is the persistence of the Millet system's principles in the region. One striking example is the application of religious law in family and personal status matters in several Middle Eastern countries. In Lebanon, for instance, religious courts preside over marriage, divorce, and inheritance issues, a direct descendent of the Ottoman approach to communal autonomy.

Delving deeper, we find that the Ottoman's pragmatic approach to governance—balancing central authority with local administration—has been mirrored in contemporary legal systems. The Empire's intricate bureaucracy and codification of laws, such as the Mecelle—a civil code that amalgamated Islamic law with European legal systems—has had a lasting impact. Modern Turkish law, for instance, has its roots in the Mecelle, and through the influence of Mustafa Kemal Atatürk, it heavily shaped the country's transition from an empire to a republic.

Yet, it would be an oversight to ignore the counterarguments suggesting that the Ottoman legal legacy is not a panacea for modern governance challenges. Critics argue that the continuation of religious courts and communal autonomy can exacerbate sectarian divisions, undermining national unity and the development of a cohesive legal system. Such fragmentation, they contend, can stifle progress and contribute to social stratification.

In response, it is essential to clarify that the Ottoman legacy is not proposed as a silver bullet but as a historical prototype that offers lessons and frameworks adaptable to contemporary needs. The system's flexibility and capacity for integrating diverse legal traditions can serve as a blueprint for creating more inclusive and representative governance structures.

Moreover, additional supporting evidence can be drawn from the realm of administrative law. The legacy of the Ottoman's "qanun," or administrative regulations, persists in the form of modern regulatory bodies that oversee various aspects of governance. These reflect the Empire's efforts to institutionalize state functions and provide a measure of predictability and order to governance.

In conclusion, the assertion that the Ottoman Empire's legal and administrative legacy continues to shape contemporary governance stands reinforced. From the persistence of religious and communal autonomy in legal matters to the enduring influence of Ottoman codification and bureaucracy, the echoes of the past reverberate through the present. It is a testament to the Empire's sophisticated approach to governance that, centuries later, its frameworks and principles remain relevant, offering a time-honored perspective on the art of statecraft.

As the sun of the Empire has set, its legacy in law and governance remains a guiding star in the firmament of the modern Middle East. It serves as a reminder that history's greatest lessons are often hidden within the folds of time, awaiting rediscovery and application by those with the vision to look beyond the immediate horizon. The Ottoman Empire's legal tapestry, rich with the threads of diversity and order, continues to provide a blueprint for governance that respects tradition while embracing the potential for progress and unity.

# Personalities of Power

## Mehmed the Conqueror

Before dawn, the world was a canvas of indigo and charcoal, speckled with the somber glow of vigilant stars. On one such morning, as the fickle breath of spring wrestled with the lingering chill of winter, a young sultan rode forth from the formidable gates of Edirne. His silhouette cut a sharp contrast against the awakening sky—a herald of the sun's imminent ascent. This was no ordinary morning, nor was this an ordinary man. This was Mehmed II, soon to be known as Mehmed the Conqueror, a man whose dreams were as vast as the empire he was destined to expand.

From his earliest days, Mehmed was sculpted by the hands of fate and ambition. His father, Murad II, was a sultan of considerable renown, but young Mehmed was not content to merely inherit; he sought to eclipse. His eyes, dark pools of resolve, seemed to reflect not the world he saw, but the world he wished to create. His tutors spoke of a mind as sharp as the scimitar he wielded—a mind that devoured history, strategy, and the lessons of empires long crumbled to dust.

As the tale unfolds, the clatter of the sultan's horse hooves against the cobblestones resonated like the beating of a war drum, each step a declaration of intent. Mehmed's pursuit was Constantinople, a city that eluded so many before him, its walls a towering challenge to his lineage's legacy. The air was tense with the promise of what was to come, and even the most hardened of his warriors felt the stirrings of something monumental on the horizon.

The weight of expectation rested heavily on Mehmed's shoulders, yet he bore it as if it were a cloak of feathers. There was a fire within him, one that consumed fear and doubt, leaving only the coals of determination. The sultan was no stranger to the whispers of his critics—those who questioned his youth, his experience, his very right to the throne—but he turned their doubt into the very fuel that powered his expansive vision.

Can the fervor of a single soul truly rewrite the pages of history? Mehmed's story, much like the empire he ruled, was an intricate tapestry of human endeavor, woven with threads of triumph and tragedy. His conquests spoke not only of military prowess but of a profound understanding of the era's geopolitical landscape. He was a patron of the arts and culture, recognizing that the strength of an empire lay not only in its armies but also in its identity, its very soul.

The siege of Constantinople would come to define Mehmed's legacy. It was an undertaking that seemed to defy the possible, a gamble that could have spelled ruin as easily as it could glory. Yet, as the cannons thundered and the walls trembled, so too did the world. The fall of the once-impregnable city marked a seismic shift in the balance of power, a turn of the tide that would ripple through the centuries.

In an unexpected twist, Mehmed's victory was not a tale of unchecked destruction. The conqueror showed a wisdom beyond his years, preserving much of the city's heritage and ensuring the safety of its inhabitants. Constantinople was to be reborn as Istanbul, a vibrant confluence of east and west, a symbol of the empire's newfound might and enlightened leadership.

What can we, as the heirs of history, learn from the story of Mehmed II? His life was a testament to the power of vision, the importance of cultural synthesis, and the relentless pursuit of ambition. It reveals the universal truth that the pages of our past are filled with figures both great and flawed, shaped by their desires and the inexorable march of time.

As the chronicle of Mehmed the Conqueror unfolds within these pages, you are invited to share in the insights of a ruler who shaped an era. Here, in the space where myth meets reality, we will walk the corridors of power, stand upon the battered ramparts of a city under siege, and delve into the mind of a sultan who was as much a visionary as he was a warrior.

What echoes of Mehmed's conquests reverberate in our modern world? How does the past inform our present? In seeking these answers, let us stride boldly into the narrative of an empire and a man who bent the arc of history with the force of their will, forever altering the record of human achievement.

## Suleiman the Magnificent

AS THE SUN CRESTED the horizon, its rays casting a golden hue over the sprawling city of Istanbul, the empire that Mehmed had so ambitiously expanded was on the cusp of an epoch that would forever engrave its name in the annals of history. The air was thick with the scent of spices from the bazaars, the clamor of merchants, and the whispers of a world on the brink of transformation. This was the dawn of Suleiman's era, an age where the Ottoman Empire would reach the zenith of its power, culture, and influence.

Suleiman I, known as 'the Magnificent' to the West and 'Kanuni' or 'the Lawgiver' to his subjects, ascended to the throne in 1520. His reign heralded a period of unparalleled prosperity and expansion, making the empire one of the foremost world powers of the 16th century. Suleiman's rule was not just a continuation of his forefathers' legacy; it was a crescendo of cultural renaissance, military conquests, and legal restructuring that would shape the course of history.

The Ottoman Empire under Suleiman's guidance witnessed significant milestones. His military campaigns extended the empire's dominion to the gates of Vienna, encompassing large swaths of the Middle East, North Africa, and Eastern Europe. The question lingers:

How did a single ruler leave such an indelible mark upon the world stage?

The answer lies not only in his military might but also in his sagacious governance. Suleiman's legal reforms earned him the title of 'the Lawgiver.' He overhauled the empire's legal system, striving for fairness and societal balance, which in turn fortified the administration and facilitated the empire's grandeur. His contributions to the legal sphere resonate even today, echoing the significance of a harmonious rule of law over an expansive and diverse empire.

Why is it crucial to understand such a towering historical figure now? Suleiman's reign exemplifies the balance between cultural patronage and military prowess, a reminder that the foundations of a powerful state are as much about governance and the arts as they are about force. In our contemporary quest for societal advancement, the echoes of Suleiman's achievements articulate the importance of visionary leadership and holistic development.

Moving from the grandeur of the past to the intricacies of the present, one cannot help but wonder about the lasting impacts of Suleiman's reign on today's geopolitical landscape. Do the borders drawn by his conquests still delineate nations and influence international politics? How do his legal reforms reflect in the current judicial systems of the nations that once formed the Ottoman mosaic?

History matters now more than ever because it holds the keys to understanding our current world—a world built upon the triumphs and tribulations of those who came before us. The Ottoman Empire, under Suleiman's rule, was a microcosm of governance, culture, and military innovation. It reminds us that the past is not merely a distant echo but a continuous melody that shapes our identity and aspirations.

## Roxelana: Power Behind the Throne

AMIDST THE GRANDEUR of Suleiman's legacy, nestled within the serpentine corridors of power, a figure of enigmatic allure and formidable influence rose to prominence. The Topkapi Palace, a sprawling complex of opulence and authority, was not solely the domain of the sultan. Within its walls, a woman of exceptional cunning and charisma wielded a power that would alter the course of the empire—her name was Hurrem Sultan, known as Roxelana in the West.

Born into obscurity, Roxelana was of Ruthenian descent, plucked from the fabric of her homeland by the tendrils of fate. She entered the Ottoman world not as a queen but as a slave, a testament to the caprices of fortune that characterized the era. Yet her ascendancy from the Sultan's concubine to his legal wife, an unprecedented leap in Ottoman imperial customs, marked the inception of a new chapter in the annals of the empire.

Suleiman, the sovereign of sea and land, faced a myriad of challenges that threatened his reign. The empire's vast territories were a breeding ground for dissent and rivalry, and the imperial court was a chessboard of political machinations. The challenge was not only to quell external threats but to navigate the intricate web of palace intrigue.

Roxelana, with her astute mind and indomitable spirit, devised a panoply of strategies to ensure her influence and secure her progeny's ascent to the throne. Her methods were manifold—she leveraged her closeness with the sultan, engaged in philanthropic works to endear herself to the public, and maneuvered her adversaries with deft political tact.

The results of her endeavors were profound. Roxelana's sons ascended to positions of power, and she herself became a central figure in the empire's political sphere. The traditional veil that had shrouded the women of the harem was lifted, and her active role in state matters defied the norms of her time. She established herself as a patron of the arts, commissioning architectural marvels such as the Haseki Sultan

Mosque, which to this day stands as a testament to her influence on the empire's cultural landscape.

Her legacy is woven with threads of ambition, love, and power. Her rise from slavery to sultana exemplifies the fluidity of social structures within the Ottoman Empire. Critics may argue that her methods were ruthless, that her ascent was marked by the downfall of others. Yet, one cannot deny the profound impact she had on the governance and cultural patronage of the era.

Visual aids, while not present in this text, would include the splendid edifices she commissioned and the intricate designs of the Ottoman court attire that she helped popularize. These tangible remnants of her influence offer a window into the world she helped shape—a world where a woman, once a slave, became the power behind the throne.

Roxelana's story is not an isolated narrative; it is inextricably linked to the overarching themes of power, culture, and the role of women in history. Her influence echoes the potential for individuals to transcend their origins and shape the world around them.

One is left to ponder: What might history look like had Roxelana not graced the stage of the Ottoman Empire? How would the cultural and political landscape have differed without her touch? Her life invites us to reflect on the interplay between fate and will, between the roles we are given and the roles we carve out for ourselves.

As the pages of history turn, the saga of Roxelana remains a captivating chapter in the story of the Ottoman Empire—a narrative that continues to inspire and provoke thought. What other shadows cast by the past still linger, shaping the present in subtle, yet indelible ways?

## Barbarossa: Admiral of the Fleet

AMID THE SHIMMERING waves of the Mediterranean, where azure skies kiss the horizon, a solitary galley cut through the water with the grace of a seabird. Its sails billowed in the wind, a triumphant symphony of canvas and rope. This vessel was no ordinary craft; it was the flagship of Hayreddin Barbarossa, the legendary Ottoman admiral whose name would become synonymous with maritime prowess and the fear of European seafarers.

On this fateful day, the air was heavy with the scent of brine and anticipation. The crew, a array of seasoned veterans and young warriors, bustled with an energy that seemed to hum through the very timbers of the ship. At the helm stood Barbarossa, his gaze fixed on the horizon, his mind as sharp as the scimitar at his side. The Mediterranean was his realm, and he its uncontested sovereign.

This was a man whose life had been a journey of survival, ambition, and destiny. Born on the island of Lesbos to a family of Greek Christian renegades, his subsequent rise to power was a tale that mirrored the transformative nature of the age. His red beard, a fiery testament to his moniker, was a banner under which men rallied and fought with the ferocity of lions.

The tale unfurled as Barbarossa, intent on capturing a formidable fortress that jealously guarded the entrance to a vital trading bay, led his fleet into battle. His ships maneuvered with an elegance that belied their lethal intent, cutting through the water towards the stone behemoth that loomed ahead. It was a dance of death and destiny, and Barbarossa was its choreographer.

The tension aboard the galley was palpable, a living thing that thrummed in the chest of each sailor. Their admiral, a man who had faced down tempests and armies alike, stood resolute, his eyes revealing the storm within. This was not just a conquest of land and treasure; it was a clash of civilizations, a moment that would define the ebb and flow of empires.

As the Ottoman vessels closed in, a sudden gust of wind caught their sails, an unexpected ally from the heavens. It was as if fate itself had declared its allegiance to the cause of Barbarossa. His men, sensing the shift, let out a roar that mingled with the roar of the cannons. It was a sound that would echo through history, a testament to their indomitable spirit.

What lessons did such a moment hold? Barbarossa's life was a mosaic of courage, cunning, and the relentless pursuit of a vision that transcended the individual. His very existence was a challenge to the status quo, a demonstration that the winds of change spared no coast, no creed, no crown.

Would you, dear reader, have the courage to set sail on such tumultuous seas? To brave the unknown for the promise of glory and the peril of defeat? The story of Barbarossa is not merely one of battles won or lost but of the human spirit's unyielding drive to master the waves of destiny.

His exploits would lead to the Ottoman control of the Mediterranean, a sea that for centuries had been the crossroads of cultures and continents. The admiral's impact on history as mentioned earlier in this book was as profound as the depths of the waters he navigated. Through his actions, he reshaped the boundaries of the known world and left an indelible mark on the records of history.

## Mustafa Kemal Atatürk

IN THE WAKE OF A LEGACY marked by formidable seafarers and emperors, the dawn of the 20th century bore witness to a figure destined to etch his name into the annals of history with a vision as clear as the Turkish skies. This man, Mustafa Kemal Atatürk, would emerge as the architect of a new epoch for the remnants of the once-mighty Ottoman Empire.

Born in 1881 in the Ottoman city of Salonika, now Thessaloniki in Greece, to a modest family, Mustafa Kemal's early life was steeped in the decline of an empire struggling to keep pace with the rapidly modernizing world. His military career began at the esteemed military academy in Istanbul, where he cultivated the skills that would later forge a nation from the ashes of an empire.

With the Empire's entry into World War I, Mustafa Kemal, then a young officer, found himself in the crucible of the Gallipoli campaign. Amidst the cacophony of gunfire and the chaos of battle, he demonstrated extraordinary leadership, earning the admiration of his men and the respect of his adversaries. Gallipoli was a turning point, not just in the war, but in the making of Mustafa Kemal as a national hero. Was it destiny or design that such a man would rise from the ranks to become a beacon of hope for his people?

The armistice that followed the end of the Great War left the Ottoman Empire dissected by foreign powers, its sovereignty in tatters. In this hour of desperation, Mustafa Kemal, now known as Atatürk, or "Father of the Turks," embarked on a quest to salvage the pride and independence of his homeland. His vision was audacious, his determination unyielding.

Atatürk's military prowess was once again on display during the Turkish War of Independence. Through a series of strategic victories, he repelled the occupying forces and laid the foundations for a sovereign Turkish state. The Treaty of Lausanne in 1923 recognized the borders of the new Republic of Turkey, and with this, a nation was reborn under Atatürk's leadership.

But what of the man beyond the uniform? The visionary who saw beyond conquests and campaigns to the heart of a modern civilization? Atatürk's reforms were as revolutionary as they were radical. He sought to transform the very fabric of Turkish society, to elevate it to the standards of contemporary Western nations. The fez, once an emblem of Ottoman identity, was cast aside in favor of Western attire. The Arabic script was replaced with the Latin alphabet to increase literacy and bridge the gap between Turkey and the West.

Atatürk's cultural revolution did not stop at superficial changes. He emancipated women, granting them unprecedented rights and access to education and professional life, challenging centuries of tradition. Religion and state were separated, as he sought to create a secular republic where governance was grounded in law and reason rather than religious edict. Each reform, each law passed, was a stroke of Atatürk's vision, painting a portrait of a nation reborn under the guiding principle: "Peace at home, peace in the world."

Yet, even icons are not immune to controversy. Atatürk's secularist policies ignited debates that have echoed through the decades. His top-down approach to modernization and the suppression of dissenting voices painted a complex picture of a leader walking the fine line between authoritarianism and progressivism. It begs the question: can the march toward progress justify the silencing of opposition?

As the sun set on the 10th of November, 1938, the final chapter of Atatürk's life came to a close. The man who had stood as the vanguard of Turkish sovereignty and modernity left behind a nation forever altered by his hand. The path he charted for Turkey, however, would continue to evolve, with successive generations interpreting Atatürk's legacy through the lens of contemporary challenges and aspirations.

Atatürk's story is one of resilience, a testament to the transformative power of vision when wielded with conviction. As the Republic of Turkey strides into the future, the echoes of Atatürk's legacy continue to resonate, reminding us that the journey of a nation is never static, but a living narrative shaped by its people and their relentless pursuit of their founding father's dream. Atatürk's life stands as a chronicle of a man who, in the face of an empire's twilight, forged a new dawn for a people determined to rise from its ashes.

# The Ottoman Empire in Literature and Arts

## Orientalism in European Art

The lure of the exotic has perennially drawn artists towards realms beyond their own borders. Within this pursuit of the unknown, the Ottoman Empire stood as a monumental source of intrigue and inspiration for European artists, especially during the 19th century. This fascination, articulated through the brush and chisel, is what we refer to as Orientalism.

Orientalism, at its essence, is the representation of Eastern societies in Western art, literature, and thought. It is often characterized by the depiction of scenes with lush and intricate detail, encapsulating aspects of life, architecture, and landscapes considered exotic by Western standards. Such portrayals, while aesthetically magnificent, frequently verge on the fantastical, capturing more the imagination of the artist than the reality of the East.

Delving deeper, Orientalism is not merely an artistic expression but also a complex and multifaceted concept that encompasses colonial attitudes, romanticized visions, and often, a profound misunderstanding of Eastern cultures. It builds on key elements such as the allure of the oriental 'Other', the West's sense of superiority, and a curious blend of fascination and fear.

Though the term 'Orientalism' was used earlier, its historical roots can be traced back to the post-medieval period when European empires began to expand their horizons. However, it was Edward Said's seminal work in 1978 that provided a critical lens to understand the underlying power dynamics and stereotypes of Orientalist thought and art.

Placing Orientalism within a broader framework, it becomes evident that this phenomenon is part of a larger pattern of cultural representation that has shaped East-West relations over centuries. It is a canvas on which the West has often projected its own desires and prejudices, clothed in the guise of admiration and intrigue.

The real-world applications of Orientalist art can be seen in the works of various European painters and sculptors who depicted the Ottoman Empire in a way that resonated with the European audience's expectations. Artists like Jean-Léon Gérôme, Eugène Delacroix, and John Frederick Lewis filled their canvases with harems, bazaars, and sultans, often emphasizing the sensuality and decadence they associated with the East.

However, it's crucial to correct some common misconceptions about Orientalism. It is not a mere celebration of Eastern beauty nor an accurate historical record of Eastern societies. Rather, it's a complex interplay of fantasy, power, and misrepresentation, with implications that reach far beyond the world of art.

What then, one might ask, is the true legacy of Orientalism in European art? Is it a window into the Western psyche, a mirror reflecting the biases of its time, or a bridge that, albeit imperfectly, connected two worlds through the power of the aesthetic?

In considering the varied sentence openers, let's evoke the atmosphere of an Orientalist painting. Imagine a bustling street in Istanbul, as painted by Delacroix. Horses prance, merchants call out their wares, and the scent of spices fills the air. Each stroke of Delacroix's brush tells a story steeped in an imagined reality, a testament to the allure of the East for the Western eye.

Should we, then, view these works as mere artifice, or can we find within them a strand of genuine appreciation and curiosity? Let's ponder this question as we explore further.

Art, after all, speaks in colors and forms where words fail. Through Orientalist art, we catch a glimpse of a conversation—a dialogue, albeit a skewed one, between cultures. It's a dialogue that continues to evolve, its language changing with the times, but its essence remains imbued with a sense of wonder and the exotic.

But let us not be seduced by mere ornamentation. Instead, let's dissect the layers, peeling back the gilded veneer to reveal the complex interplay of power and perception.

Orientalist art, with its vivid imagery and bold characters, beckons us to look closer. A single line of paint, a solitary figure in a bazaar, a fleeting glance shared between figures in a painting—each serves as an emissary from a world that once was, but perhaps only in the imaginations of those who depicted it.

In conclusion, as we embrace the simplicity of language, we recognize that the story of Orientalism in European art is not one of clarity, but one of contrasts and contradictions. It is a dance of light and shadow, where the rhythm and cadence of cultural interplay create a narrative that is as beguiling as it is contentious.

Interspersed with quotations from the artists themselves, we find a dialogue that is rich and multifaceted. Delacroix once said, "The source of my inspiration is not the imitation of nature but the spirit of the East." This statement encapsulates the essence of Orientalism—a spirit captured, not through the lens of accuracy, but through the brushstrokes of perception.

And so, with a final flourish, we show, rather than tell, the enduring impact of the Ottoman Empire on European art. It is a legacy that continues to captivate, challenge, and illuminate the corridors of history, inviting us to explore the depths of our collective imaginations.

## Ottoman Poetry and Literature

IN THE REALM OF INTELLECTUAL and cultural achievements, the Ottoman Empire boasts a legacy as enduring as its once-expansive territories. Among the empire's most profound contributions is the rich tradition of Ottoman poetry and literature, woven from the threads of diverse influences, languages, and themes. This tradition speaks not only to the heart of Ottoman society but also serves as a beacon illuminating the empire's soul.

The profound impact of poetry and literature within the Ottoman Empire cannot be overstated. It was both a reflection of the empire's intricate cultural fabric and a means of reinforcing social norms and expressing political aspirations. The verses that flowed from the pens of Ottoman poets were as varied as the empire's vast dominions, with each poet leaving an indelible mark upon the literary landscape.

The Ottoman literary canon is a cornucopia of distinguished poets and authors. Each, in their own right, carved a niche through their eloquent articulation of thoughts and emotions that continue to resonate across time. The forthcoming list is not merely a roll call but a gateway into the essence of the Ottoman spirit.

The annals of Ottoman literature are replete with luminaries such as Bâkî, Nef'i, Nedim, and Fuzûlî. These poets, among others, created works that transcended the mere beauty of form, encompassing profound philosophical musings, courtly love, and societal commentary.

Bâkî – The Sultan of Poets

Bâkî stands as a colossus in the pantheon of Ottoman poets. His mastery of language and the depth of his poetry earned him the moniker "Sultan of Poets." His life and works offered a window into the soul of the empire, capturing the grandeur and pathos of his time. Originally known as Mahmud Abdülbâkî, but better known as Bâkî, was a poet of the 16th century whose verse was marked by innovative use of language and thematic depth. He served under Suleiman the Magnificent, a period often regarded as the zenith of Ottoman cultural development. Bâkî's poetry, replete with mystical undertones, explored the ephemeral nature of life and the pursuit of divine love. Bâkî's divan, a collection of his poetry, offers an expansive testament to his skill. His famed qasida, an ode to Sultan Suleiman upon the conquest of Sigetvar, exemplifies his ability to intertwine political triumph with spiritual introspection. His work garnered praise not only from his contemporaries but also from successive generations who viewed his poetry as a benchmark for literary excellence. Bâkî's influence extended beyond the realm of literature, shaping the Ottoman court's perception of the poet's role within society. His verses became a model for ceremonial poetry, setting a standard for how events and figures of significance were commemorated in verse. While Bâkî's poetry echoed the grandeur of the imperial court, other poets turned their gaze upon the subtleties of human experience and emotion, crafting verses that spoke to the soul's intimate corridors.

Nef'i – The Sharp Tongued Satirist

Nef'i, known for his biting satires, wielded his pen with a ferocity that often provoked the ire of the powerful. His candid observations on corruption and hypocrisy within the Ottoman elite make his work an invaluable chronicle of his era's societal undercurrents. Ömer Nef'i, active during the early 17th century, was a poet whose satirical verses spared no one, not even the sultan. His sharp wit and fearless criticism of political and social malaise afforded him a contentious but significant role in Ottoman literature. It was his unapologetic candor that ultimately led to his execution, yet it is that very audacity that cements his legacy. The potency of Nef'i's satirical poetry is evidenced by the threats it posed to those in power. His works serve as historical documents, offering scholars and enthusiasts a glimpse into the political and social dynamics of his times. His critiques are peppered with pungent humor and incisive commentary, a combination that ensures his place in Ottoman literary history. Nef'i's satires became a medium through which societal grievances could be articulated. His verses offered an outlet for public sentiment, serving as a precursor to the watchdog role that literature can play in society.

While satire provided a lens through which to scrutinize society, other poets sought to capture the ephemeral beauty of life and love through a more lyrical and aesthetically pleasing approach.

Nedim – The Lyricist of Istanbul

Nedim brought a new color to Ottoman poetry with his lyrical depictions of Istanbul's daily life. His work is characterized by an effervescent joy and a celebration of the city's vibrant culture during the Tulip Era. A poet of the 18th century,Nedim is celebrated for his pioneering use of a simpler, more conversational language in his poetry, which was a departure from the highly stylized and Persian-influenced court poetry of his predecessors. His verses sang of the pleasures of Istanbul, its gardens, and its social gatherings, reflecting the joie de vivre of the Tulip Era. His poetry, particularly his gazels (lyric poems), is imbued with vivid imagery that transports the reader to the heart of Ottoman urban life. Contemporary accounts praise Nedim for capturing the zeitgeist of his time in a manner that was accessible and delightful to a broad audience. Nedim's work illustrates the transformative power of literature to act as a cultural repository, preserving the nuances of a particular time and place. His portrayal of Istanbul during the Tulip Era provides historians and readers with a rich tapestry of urban Ottoman culture.

From the bustling streets of Istanbul, we turn inward to the contemplative and spiritual verses that sought to express the inexpressible mysteries of love and divine longing.

Fuzûlî – The Poet of Love and Longing

Fuzûlî's poetry is a testament to the profound emotional and spiritual dimensions of Ottoman verse. His exploration of love, loss, and existential yearning resonates with a timeless universality. A 16th-century poet who wrote in Azerbaijani, Persian, and Arabic, Fuzûlî is best known for his work "Leyla and Majnun," a poetic rendition of a classic love story that has become synonymous with the expression of passionate, unattainable love. His verses delve into the pain of separation and the quest for union with the beloved, whether human or divine. Fuzûlî's poetry has been celebrated for its emotional depth and its masterful interweaving of secular and spiritual themes. His work not only stands as a pinnacle of Ottoman literature but also resonates with the shared human experience of love and longing. The legacy of Fuzûlî's poetry lies in its universal appeal. It transcends cultural and temporal boundaries, capturing the essence of human desire and its intersection with the spiritual quest. His work continues to inspire artists and poets worldwide, demonstrating the enduring power of literature to touch the deepest aspects of our humanity.

As we traverse the rich landscape of Ottoman poetry and literature, it becomes clear that each poet, with their distinct voice and vision, contributed to a complex and vibrant mosaic.

In conclusion, Ottoman poetry and literature is not merely a historical curiosity but a living tradition that continues to enchant and inform. Through the verses of its poets, the empire speaks, reminding us of the enduring power of words to shape, reflect, and transcend the human experience. Ottoman poets, with their diverse perspectives and profound insights, have bequeathed to us a literary heritage that invites us to explore, reflect, and, ultimately, to understand the depth of our own existence.

As we ponder the legacy of Ottoman poetry and literature, let us remember the words of Fuzûlî, who once wrote, "Love is not to be reasoned away." In this simple yet profound statement, we find the essence of all poetry—a truth that, through the beauty of its expression, reaches beyond reason to touch the soul.

## The Empire on Screen

THE OTTOMAN EMPIRE, a sprawling domain that once stretched across three continents, has long fascinated historians, scholars, and artists alike. Its rich history, marked by grand conquests, monumental architecture, and a mosaic of cultures, has been a wellspring of inspiration for visual storytelling. The portrayal of this empire in film and television provides a unique lens through which to view its legacy—a medium that can captivate audiences, shape perceptions, and influence collective memory.

The allure of the Ottoman Empire's grand narrative has not been lost on filmmakers and showrunners, who have sought to capture its essence on screen. The depiction of this empire through visual media is not merely a matter of entertainment; it serves as an imperative conduit for cultural transmission and historical reflection. In examining the representation of the Ottoman Empire in film and television, one must consider the fidelity of these portrayals to historical facts, the creative liberties taken for the sake of drama, and the impact these interpretations have on our understanding of the past.

When setting the parameters for such an analysis, it is crucial to consider the historical accuracy, cultural representation, narrative context, and artistic interpretation. These criteria allow for a comprehensive exploration of how the Ottoman Empire is brought to life on screen and to what extent these portrayals resonate with the truth of its history.

Films like "Lawrence of Arabia" (1962) and "The Ottoman Lieutenant" (2017) juxtapose sharply in their portrayal of the empire—both in terms of historical perspective and cultural nuance. While "Lawrence of Arabia" presents the Ottoman forces as adversaries during the Arab Revolt, "The Ottoman Lieutenant" offers a more romanticized view of the empire through the eyes of an American nurse and her love affair with an Ottoman officer.

Similarities between the two are found in their epic scale, their treatment of war, and their use of the empire as a backdrop for personal and political drama. However, the contrast is equally significant; "Lawrence of Arabia" is criticized for its Orientalist perspective and simplification of complex political dynamics, whereas "The Ottoman Lieutenant" is often scrutinized for glossing over the Armenian

Genocide—a glaring omission that has sparked controversy and debate.

Television series like "Magnificent Century" (2011-2014), a Turkish production that dramatizes the reign of Sultan Suleiman the Magnificent, provide a contrast to Western cinematic interpretations. The show's popularity in Turkey and abroad is indicative of a fascination with the imperial court's opulence and intrigue. Yet, despite its appeal, the series has faced criticism for its historical inaccuracies and melodramatic embellishments, which often overshadow the more profound aspects of the era's political and cultural transformations.

The visual aids of costume, set design, and cinematography are instrumental in distinguishing these portrayals. They serve as silent storytellers that can either reinforce historical authenticity or perpetuate stereotypes. The lavish costumes of "Magnificent Century," for instance, do more than clothe actors; they evoke the splendor of the Ottoman court. In contrast, the arid landscapes and battle-worn uniforms in "Lawrence of Arabia" convey the brutal reality of desert warfare and colonial tensions.

What do these comparisons reveal? They underscore the delicate balance between historical documentation and narrative artistry. The broader implications of this analysis touch upon the enduring struggle between presenting a historically accurate account and crafting a compelling story that resonates with modern audiences.

The relevance of these portrayals in contemporary times cannot be overstated. In an era where media consumption is at an all-time high, the images and narratives projected on screens play a pivotal role in shaping our understanding of history. With each depiction, the Ottoman Empire is reimagined and reinterpreted, its legacy reframed for a new generation of viewers.

But what is the cost of such reinterpretation? Does the simplification of history for the sake of a gripping plot undermine the complexity of the empire's narrative? Can the artistic embellishment of the past serve to enlighten or does it risk perpetuating misconceptions?

The challenge lies in bridging the gap between cinematic spectacle and historical substance—a task that demands meticulous research, cultural sensitivity, and artistic integrity. As viewers, we must navigate these on-screen representations with a critical eye, recognizing the interplay between fact and fiction, and appreciating the power of film and television to transport us to different times and places while reflecting on their authenticity and intent.

In conclusion, the portrayal of the Ottoman Empire on screen is a mirror reflecting the aspirations and anxieties of both its creators and its audiences. From the windswept deserts of Arabia to the grandeur of the Topkapi Palace, these visual narratives invite us to ponder the empire's enduring enigma. They challenge us to question, to learn, and ultimately, to understand the nuanced history that continues to shape the world we live in today. As we immerse ourselves in these cinematic journeys, let us recall the words of the great Ottoman poet Fuzûlî: "Love is not to be reasoned away," and neither is the allure of the empire's storied past, which, like love itself, continues to captivate and compel us, beyond the confines of the screen.

## Music of the Empire

THE RESONANT STRINGS of the oud; the haunting call of the ney; the rhythmic beat of the kudüm – these are but a whisper of the past, echoes of the Ottoman Empire's vast cultural panorama. Music, an integral facet of this bygone realm, offers a profound window into the soul of its people and their history. It is in the interlacing melodies and rhythms where one can seek the essence of the empire's musical heritage, a symphony of influences and instruments that orchestrated a unique and enduring soundscape.

Drawing from its geographical expanse, the Ottoman Empire was a crucible for a variety of musical traditions. Its sound was as diverse as its population, encompassing the intricate Arab maqams, the melodic scales of Persian radifs, and the rhythmic complexities of Balkan folk. The resulting synthesis was a music that was both rich and nuanced, capable of expressing the full range of human emotions.

But what were the pillars upon which this aural edifice stood? To grasp the full scope of Ottoman music, one must delve into the traditional ensembles known as 'mehter,' the courtly music that graced the halls of sultans.

The mehter bands, with their thunderous drums and piercing zurnas, were not merely musical troupes; they were symbols of power and prestige. Their martial tunes, with origins traced to Central Asia, stirred the hearts of soldiers and instilled fear in the hearts of foes. Can one imagine the sight of Janissaries marching to battle, the air trembling with the sound of the mehterhane, embodying the might of the empire?

Within the serene gardens and opulent chambers of the sultan's palace, a different musical tradition flourished. Here, the refined sounds of the 'fasıl' ensemble played, crafting an ambiance of elegance and artistry. The fasıl, a suite of vocal and instrumental pieces, was performed by virtuosos whose talents were as revered as the poets and painters of the court.

But beyond the pomp and ceremony, there lay the spiritual realm of Ottoman music. The Sufi orders, with their mystical practices, embraced music as a means to divine communion. The ney, an end-blown reed flute, became more than an instrument; it was a voice crying in the wilderness, a symbol of the soul's yearning for the eternal. The famed poet and musician, Dede Efendi, with his soul-stirring compositions, captured this yearning in notes that seemed to transcend the mortal sphere.

One cannot discuss Ottoman music without mentioning the 'makam' system, the modal structure that underpinned its melodies. Each makam, with its specific intervals and patterns, was a world unto itself, capable of conveying a spectrum of moods and emotions. Were the listeners of old not transported by the plaintive strains of the Hicaz makam, or enlivened by the joyous leaps of the Rast?

The instruments, too, were as varied as the empire itself. The qanun with its trapezoidal body and plucked strings; the rebab, ancestor of the modern violin; the darbuka, with its goblet-shaped drum – these were the tools with which musicians painted auditory landscapes. Even today, one can hear the legacy of these instruments in the streets of Istanbul, a testament to their timeless appeal.

What can statistics tell us about the spread of these musical traditions? The Ottoman Empire, at its zenith, spanned three continents, and its music seeped into the cultural fabric of countless communities. It influenced the classical traditions of Europe, where composers like Mozart and Beethoven at times incorporated Turkish-inspired themes into their works. It is said by some that the Janissary bands were the precursors to the Western military bands, their instruments and music leaving an indelible mark on the sounds of martial music.

In discussing these art forms, it is crucial to clarify terms that might perplex the uninitiated. What is a 'makam'? How does it differ from the Western scale? A makam is defined by a set of rules that governs its melody, including the notes used, their range, and the progression in which they should be played. Unlike the Western scale, which typically consists of seven notes, a makam can have microtones – notes that exist between the standard notes, offering a greater depth of expression.

As we look back at the history of Ottoman music, the key takeaways are its diversity, its ability to unify various cultural strands, and its enduring legacy. The empire might have faded into the past, but its music continues to resonate, a bridge across time that connects us to a world both magnificent and mysterious.

One might ask themselves, does the music of the past hold relevance in our modern lives? Can the melodies that once echoed through the courts and camps of an ancient empire still stir the hearts of today's listeners? The answer lies not in words, but in the experience – in the closing of one's eyes, the opening of one's ears, and the letting go of time as the music of the empire takes hold. It is here, in the space between notes, where one might just find the echo of a bygone era, waiting to be rediscovered.

# Note to the reader

Thank you for purchasing this book on the history of the Ottoman Empire. While some facts may have been lost to time, we have tried to be faithful to the empire that once stood many years ago. Feel free to continue the series, as we continue looking into the ancient empires of the world. If you truly have enjoyed reading this book, don't just leave a review, tell others about it.

# Don't miss out!

Visit the website below and you can sign up to receive emails whenever History Nerds publishes a new book. There's no charge and no obligation.

https://books2read.com/r/B-A-ODOK-QPJTC

**BOOKS2READ**

Connecting independent readers to independent writers.

# Also by History Nerds

**Ancient Empires**
The Ottoman Empire
Rome: The Rise and Fall


**Celtic Heroes and Legends**
Celtic History
William Butler Yeats: Nobel Prize Winning Poet
Robert the Bruce
Scáthach
Finn McCool
William Wallace: Scotland's Great Freedom Fighter


**Frauen des Krieges**
Boudica: Königin der Icener
Jeanne d'Arc
Irena Sendler


**Great Wars of the World**

World War 1
World War 2
The Napoleonic Wars: One Shot at Glory
The Serbian Revolution: 1804-1835
Peace Won by the Saber: The Crimean War, 1853-1856
The Fiery Maelstrom of Freedom
The Wars of the Roses

**Pirate Chronicles**
Grace O'Malley: The Pirate Queen of Ireland
Blackbeard
William Kidd

**The History of the Vikings**
Vikings
Longships on Restless Seas

**Women of War**
Boudica: Queen of the Iceni
Joan of Arc
Irena Sendler
Virginia Hall
Queen Amanirenas

**World History**
The History of the United Kingdom

The History of Ireland
The History of America
The History of Scotland
The History of Wales


**Standalone**
Grace O'Malley: Die Piratenkönigin von Irland